The E–Mail Diet Book

Martin A. Siegel and Steven E. Clapp

Practical advice on shedding
those unsightly pounds of e-mail that
fill your memory and consume your time.
Use the tremendous power of e-mail to achieve
your personal and professional objectives.

The E–Mail Diet Book
Martin A. Siegel and Steven E. Clapp

Quantity discounts are available from the publisher for use of this book in business and educational institutions. For further information, contact LifeQuest, 6404 S. Calhoun Street, Fort Wayne, Indiana 46807, or call 1–800–774–3360.

Every effort has been made to verify the accuracy of information in this book, but the pace of change in hardware, software, and service providers is so rapid that some descriptive information about particular products and services inevitably changes between the time a book like this is written and the day the completed product comes out of the book bindery. For the most current information on specific products and services, visit www.emaildietbook.com, the authors' website.

The authors of this book have strong opinions about many matters of corporate e-mail policy, privacy issues, and a whole lot of other things that have nothing to do with e-mail. They are, however, not attorneys and have never been mistaken for attorneys. Information in this book concerning the legal aspects of e-mail, privacy, and corporate policy is not a substitute for consultation with your attorney. The authors are also not physicians; follow their counsel on physical weight loss entirely at your own risk!

ISBN 1–893270–26–2

Library of Congress Control Number: 2005936465

Contents

The authors of this book are, on most days of the week, pleasant, friendly people with decent communication skills. If you pay them and feed them well, they can conduct workshops and seminars without putting people to sleep. If you would like information about their availability for a workshop or seminar in your organization, go to their website at www.emaildietbook.com or contact them by e-mail at martysiegel@gmail.com (Marty Siegel) or steveneclapp@gmail.com (Steve Clapp).

*The romance of the Net came not from how
it was built or how it worked but from how it
was used. . . . America's romance with the
highway system, by analogy, was created
not so much by the first person who figured
out how to grade a road or make blacktop or
paint a stripe down the middle but by the
first person who discovered you could drive
a convertible down Route 66 like James Dean
and play your radio loud and have a good
time.*

Katie Hafner & Matthew Lyon
Where Wizards Stay Up Late

*E-mail is such an integral part of business and
everyday life today that we tend to forget how
recently it became popular. . . . Yet e-mail's
popularity has produced one very troubling
side effect: spam. Unsolicited e-mail is a
spreading plague that feeds off the unique
power of the Internet to connect hundreds of
millions of computer users around the world,
at virtually no cost.*

Bill Gates
June 24, 2003 Essay

*Context communicates volumes–but e-mail lacks
context. Nuance and emphasis are missing; a
direct message can sound cold; your gentle
joke can be missed because the recipient cannot
see your tongue in your cheek.*

Harry Beckwith
What Clients Love

Chapter One
E-Mail, Dieting, and Chocolate

"He's done it to me again," Steve said to his wife Sara on a Sunday afternoon. She, Steve, and Marty had just finished having brunch together. "He's got me chasing a rabbit. I've got four research projects and three books in process; a calendar jammed with workshops and consultations; and he's got me seriously considering the possibility of collaborating on a book about e-mail."

"It wasn't exactly like he twisted your arm," she observed with an 'I've got you figured out' look on her face.

"Of course not. I could resist that. He's got my mind hooked — the same thing he did to me at two o'clock in the morning when we were roommates in college. He'd spin out this new perspective or vision of something, and I'd ignore the paper I was writing or the exam I was studying for and start chasing the intellectual rabbit with him."

"Well, the two of you think so much alike that it's probably dangerous. You got me pulled into it too. He threw out the idea, you started talking about how to develop it, and then all three of us were brainstorming book titles."

"That doesn't mean we're going to do the book though," Steve added.

"Yes it does. I know that look," Sara replied.

And obviously we did the book. The fact that you are reading this makes you part of the dialogue that we started that day.

Electronic mail, or e-mail, is a relatively simple concept made possible by advances in electronic media which would have sounded like science fiction to earlier generations. Instead of using paper, we compose e-mail messages on computers and send them electronically to other computers. Those who receive our e-mail messages use an e-mail program to read them and, if desired, to respond to us. With computer devices becoming smaller and smaller, e-mail can now be sent using cell phones, personal digital assistants (PDAs), or similar tools in addition to traditional computers.

Estimates of e-mail use are staggering and increasing all the time. The most recent estimate we've read is that over 150 million people use e-mail and send over 20 billion messages a day. One survey of major companies in New York City found that people were receiving an average of 80 e-mail messages a day. Those figures will be low by the time this book is in print. Current estimates are that 55 billion e-mail messages will be sent each day in 2007.

The CEO of an agribusiness sent an e-mail to all employees around the world to reassure them about anxiety over anthrax. He received a staggering 1,000 responses, which kept him busy for four evenings at home. Many people routinely receive over a hundred e-mails a day — some business, some personal, and some unwanted.

Steve sent an e-mail to a few friends seeking chocolate recipes for a booklet to be given away at a Taste of Chocolate event that was raising money to feed the hungry. He was seeking perhaps ten recipes; he received over two hundred, most of which were sent to him by people he did not know who learned about the search. Six of the recipes came from people in other countries! The recipes are still coming as this book goes to press, and you'll find a few of them incorporated into the text. (We guarantee little in this book, but we absolutely guarantee these recipes will not help you lose weight!)

E-mail has become an important mode of communication for millions of people in large corporations, government institutions, small businesses, universities and colleges, elementary schools and high schools, churches and other nonprofit organizations, and private homes. Hundreds of books have been written to tell you about various aspects of e-mail. We've purchased and read many of them ourselves.

But not many books that we've read tell you in a concise way how to handle e-mail — how to make the most of it without being overwhelmed by it. That was the issue that started this project. Marty handles e-mail primarily through a university-maintained network with the help of Microsoft Outlook. Steve receives and handles e-mail primarily through America Online but has also used Eudora and Outlook Express. Sara works through a business-maintained network with Lotus Notes. All three of us have had times when we were swamped by the volume of e-mail we had to process. All three of us have returned to our workplaces from relatively short personal or business trips to find the e-mail messages waiting for us numbering not in the dozens but in the hundreds and even thousands.

The volume of unsolicited e-mail, or spam, has become truly overwhelming. Because e-mail is so cheap and so easy to send, huge volumes are sent by individuals and companies seeking to make money. It's what would happen to postal service mail (or snail mail) if paper, printing, and postage were free to everyone. Ferris Research estimates that spam costs $10 billion a year in the United States alone in tiny bits of computer power and the value of wasted time, multiplied by millions of users. The Radicati Group estimates the worldwide cost at $20.5 billion.

E-mail is a tremendously powerful medium, but it can also be an overwhelming and even addictive medium. As we visited together during that Sunday brunch, we increasingly realized that we and many others need practical strategies for handling e-mail. It seemed that our electronic mailboxes, e-mail lists, and e-mail files were obese. We recognized that we needed to go on e-mail diets and get back to the place where we were in control of our e-mail rather than being controlled by it. In the process, we've also discovered many ways to make more effective use of the e-mail medium in our personal and professional lives. Now with the zealousness of those who have successfully gone through a dieting program, we want to share our strategies with you.

In our increasingly computer-oriented culture, there seem to be two categories of people who can benefit from the strategies proposed in this book. First, there are those like ourselves who spend much of their time working with computers and who embrace the technology (though not always without apprehension). Many of us work or volunteer or find recreation in settings where large numbers of people choose e-mail as a preferred means of communication. Our electronic mailboxes grow fat with messages, and we sometimes spend an unhealthy proportion of our days responding to those e-mail communications. We appreciate the power and efficiency of the medium, but we also feel like e-mail controls us rather than empowers us. E-mail causes considerable anxiety for many of us—anxiety about spam, anxiety about identity theft, anxiety about unanswered e-mail, and anxiety about e-mail keeping us from accomplishing more important tasks. We need a weight-loss plan that puts us in control.

Second, there are those who aren't yet comfortable with computers in general or with e-mail in particular. Word processing, databases, spreadsheets, e-mail, the World Wide Web, and related applications seem intimidating. From the perspective of e-mail consumption, these persons are too thin and need some good protein-mix and high tech-carbohydrates to help them take advantage of the opportunities open to us today. Unfortunately, many people work in settings where it isn't acceptable to say that they don't feel at home with the technology, so there is little choice but to stay in the closet with their e-mail phobia.

We've written this book to help people in both categories. We believe that you'll find this book characterized by:

- An emphasis on strategies rather than on every detail of every e-mail system on the market. Those details change, but the strategies can work for you for your e-mail lifetime.

- An approach to e-mail strategies that has much in common with some of the best approaches to time management and priority setting. Just as time management strategies strive to help you gain control over your time and schedule, we want to help you take control of your e-mail—to protect your time and also to help you harness the power of the medium.

- An effort to communicate in simple, straightforward language rather than esoteric, technological jargon. We know this runs the risk of irritating a few people who will feel that our language could at times be more precise. If you are in that group of people, we hope you will cut us some slack. We want this book to be useful to those who want the power and communication potential of electronic media but are not interested in the terminology or the technology underlying that media.

- An intentional plan to have fun with the dieting analogy. We'll try not to get too cute as we proceed, but we want the book to be fun to write and fun to read. We'll also make it clear when we're serious about the importance of particular strategies. (And we mean no offense to those persons who have real eating disorders.)

- An effort to name and deal with some of the managerial and ethical issues facing companies, government and nonprofit organizations, and networks in dealing with the growing volume of e-mail. We'll talk about the ethical and practical issues related to spam (e-mail that you don't want to receive) and phishing (identity theft) and offer strategies for handling these continuing problems.

- A desire to be in continuing communication with those who read the book. We'd like to hear from you about ways in which the book has been helpful and about ways in which it could have been even more helpful. Please let us hear from you at our website or at our e-mail addresses (put "e-mail diet" in the subject line):

Website:	www.emaildietbook.com
Marty Siegel:	martysiegel@gmail.com
Steve Clapp:	steveneclapp@gmail.com

- An effort to let you know when you may want to skip a particular section because it does not apply to you or is likely to repeat information you already possess if you are an experienced computer user. We'll also highlight sections that seem to us especially important (though we hope you will want to devour every word of the book!).

At the end of the book are appendices containing some very basic information for readers who have little or no familiarity at all with e-mail or Internet use. Appendix A, "Understanding the Basics of E-Mail," explains the steps involved in composing, sending, and reading e-mail messages, and a description of some common uses of e-mail. Appendix B, "Options in Internet Service Providers," describes some issues that new users of e-mail and the Internet may want to consider when choosing a means for connecting to the World Wide Web.

Cranberry Chocolate Truffles

1-1/4 c. fresh cranberries   1/2 c. light corn syrup
12 oz. semisweet chocolate pieces   1/4 c. evaporated milk
1/8 tsp. cayenne pepper   2 tsp. vanilla extract
1/4 c. each cocoa powder and powdered sugar to coat

Prepare an 8" x 8" pan by lining with clear wrap. Pulse cranberries in a blender for 10 seconds. In a medium saucepan, bring the cranberries and corn syrup to a boil, and boil for 5–7 minutes stirring occasionally until the liquid is reduced. Remove from heat. Add chocolate pieces and stir until chocolate is completely melted. Add remaining ingredients and stir vigorously until the mixture is thick and glossy. Pour into the pan and refrigerate for one hour.

Using a melon baller or teaspoon, scoop chocolate mixture into a small portions onto a baking sheet lined with parchment paper. Refrigerate for 15 minutes. Sift the cocoa powder and powdered sugar together and place mixture into a shallow dish or pie plate. Roll the chocolate portions into balls and drop into cocoa mixture, rolling each to coat. Chill until firm. Store in an airtight container in the refrigerator up to two weeks. Remove from refrigerator one hour before serving.

                                        Sara Sprunger Clapp

Chapter Two
Too Fat or Too Thin with E-Mail?
Coming Out of the Closet
with E-Mail Disorders!

- *This is pretty embarrassing. I'm sure that you sent me an answer to my question by e-mail, but I think I deleted it. I came back from a meeting on the West Coast, and I had page after page of new e-mail messages to process. I started reading and then realized that I was never going to get done. I finally just gave up and deleted everything. Then, after wiping all of them out, I realized that you and a couple of other people were going to get back to me by e-mail.*

- *I'm driven by e-mail. In our office, we have this network system that lets us know when we receive a new piece of e-mail. Every time I get a new piece, I feel like it's a phone call – I should do something about it right away. I stop what I'm doing, go to my electronic mailbox, read the e-mail, and try to respond to it. I may do that twenty times during a day, and I know it's keeping me from completing some important projects.*

- *Don't use my name if you put this in your book. I have no clue how to handle e-mail. I have my secretary take care of it just like my other correspondence. I have her print off the e-mail messages for me, and then I dictate my replies into a recorder. She types up my responses and then sends them by e-mail. I rarely use the computer myself. I've got to change though. My president would be furious if he knew that I wasn't responding directly by computer. He's already unhappy that it takes me so long to answer e-mail. I still use a full-time secretary, but our president doesn't.*

- *My software program saves the e-mail I receive unless I intentionally delete it. I have so much saved e-mail now that I couldn't even estimate the volume. It must take up several megabytes on my hard drive. I know hard drive space is cheap, but I can't find anything. I go back to look for an e-mail that raised some kind of policy question, and I may end up looking at a few thousand pieces of old e-mail before I find it or give up.*

- *I bought this computer and started using e-mail so I could stay in touch with my grandchildren. It's worked very well for that, but I find myself angry about the volume of spam I receive. I don't appreciate daily offers for Viagra and increasing the size of my husband's genitals. My credit rating doesn't need to be repaired, and I don't need a second mortgage or life insurance. And I know that I'm failing to take advantage of what I could be doing through e-mail and the Internet.*

When talking with people we trust, an increasing number of us admit that we need to improve how we handle e-mail. That's what this book is about. Someone may get a chuckle out of seeing you holding *The E-Mail Diet Book*, but watch out—the person who is laughing the hardest will be the one who steals it.

Most of us are never fully satisfied with our physical appearance. Some of us think we're too fat—some too thin. Diet books and diet programs and diet support groups abound. One member of this writing team has tried several of them. The other half of the writing team was once thirty-five pounds underweight, which is an eating disorder of another kind. As we've looked at diet books and plans, we've continued to observe some interesting similarities to problems with e-mail. Here they are:

1. Dieting issues pervade our entire culture, and the same is increasingly true of computers and e-mail. Try picking up a Sunday newspaper that has nothing in it about diet, weight loss, or exercise. You can't. And you also can't find a Sunday newspaper without something in it about computers. In his classic book *The Third Wave*, Alvin Toffler predicted years ago that computers and electronic communication would change our society more profoundly than anything since the industrial revolution. He was right.

2. Just as weight loss is more talked about than accomplished, so too are improvements in the way we use time and computers. "More people will start a diet tomorrow than today!" And more people will make changes in their use of time and computers tomorrow than today. We know something needs to be done, but it's so tempting to delay! We tend to think of things outside of our computer life when looking at time management, but that misses a major consumer of time—and a major resource in saving time. Just talking about it, however, isn't enough. With most people in business, university, and nonprofit settings spending two hours a day or more working with e-mail, we need to take action. If you can save thirty minutes a day in handling e-mail, you'll gain 125 hours a year—more than three forty-hour work weeks. That's a very significant amount of time. And if you use e-mail to its best advantage, you may be able to share information in ways that generate significant gains for your organization or for your own life.

3. **As with diets, there's a lot of conflicting advice concerning computers and e-mail.** Do an Internet search on the words *fat, obesity, diet,* or *nutrition,* and you'll find a staggering number of sites and suggestions for losing weight. Some diets say to raise your protein and carbohydrate consumption and dramatically lower your fat consumption. Some say that carbohydrates are the real problem and that you don't have to be all that worried about fat. Some say that keeping a certain ratio among protein, carbohydrates, and fat is the answer.

Some authorities suggest that fatness isn't as important as fitness. Have you heard about the fruit test for fitness? If you look like an apple with weight around the middle, you're in trouble; if you look like a pear with weight around your hips and thighs, you are probably carrying more "good fat." Good fat, bad fat, good cholesterol, bad cholesterol, waist to hip ratios—ACK! Who can keep up with it? Sorting out all the advice on weight loss is no easy task.

The fast pace of change in computer technology and our increasing reliance on e-mail has also produced a vast amount of perplexing and sometimes downright conflicting advice. For example:

- "Only a fool wastes money on a service like America Online. The average person can do everything needed with a Yahoo or Hotmail account."

- "A service like America Online makes it much easier for the average person to use e-mail and the Net."

- "Gmail (Google mail) is the wave of the future. It's worth every second of the time it takes to learn how it works."

15

- "Don't waste your money buying a software package to handle e-mail; that's more than you need. It will take you twice as long to learn how to use it as to learn a simple system that comes with your computer or from an Internet service provider."

- "Companies must not permit employees to use e-mail for any personal matters. Personal use of e-mail can cost the company a fortune in employee time and computer disk space."

- "Companies should view personal use of e-mail like they view personal phone calls. Letting people use e-mail for a few personal matters is a way to give a fringe benefit that isn't expensive since the computers are there anyway. Besides that, you can't successfully enforce a policy against personal use of e-mail unless you become Big Brother."

- "You need to use a filtering system to control spam. The rules that you form with a program like Outlook Express can keep most unwanted e-mail away from you."

- "Filtering programs and rules have their own problems. They can't divert all unwanted e-mail, but they may keep you from receiving some e-mail that you want. You're better off to make good use of the DELETE key on your computer."

4. As with diets, it's easy to focus on the next thing coming—the next bite (byte)—rather than noting the cumulative effect. We overeat, in part, because we don't stop to assess the result of what we're doing. Interaction with computers can be very similar. If we're on a network which immediately informs us that we've received e-mail, we interrupt our work in progress to read the e-mail. If the default in our e-mail software is to save e-mail messages unless we proactively delete them, we tend to save them.

Many of us are increasingly sending one another files that are attached to e-mail, such as pictures of grandchildren, scanned articles to read, word processing documents to review, spreadsheets with financial facts or projections, and databases (of potential customers, mailing lists, or other information). Many of these attachments are valuable to us on either a personal or a business level. They also take time to download and require space on the hard disk or network for storage. Even though the cost of the storage space is increasingly low, the volume of files saved can make it difficult to find what you want unless you have a clear system. Sophisticated search software helps, but nothing replaces having an organizational system that works for you. And attachments to e-mails are one of the most common ways that viruses infect computers.

The fact that e-mail communication is relatively inexpensive compared to putting stamps on envelopes or paying for long distance phone calls furthers our use of the medium. How inexpensive e-mail communication really is can be debated. It's difficult to determine what proportion of the cost of a computer, a modem, a printer, software packages, and Internet service provider fees results from e-mail. For the employee who can't accomplish his or her job without a computer regardless of e-mail usage, e-mail may be a significant fringe benefit which costs the company little additional money. For the person who purchases a computer and signs up with an Internet Service Provider (ISP) like America Online or Earthlink primarily for the purpose of staying in touch with family members through e-mail, the cost may seem higher. Some providers of e-mail service like Yahoo and Hotmail do not have a fee. On the other hand, direct cable connections and DSL to the Internet are still costly in some parts of the country, though prices are dropping.

5. Articles and books give more attention to efforts at weight loss than to efforts at weight gain, even though bulimia and anorexia are serious problems; it's tempting in a book like this to talk more about management of high volumes of e-mail than to share strategies for those needing to increase their use of the medium. While being overwhelmed with e-mail means management strategies are in order, it's also important to be aware that many of us are not taking sufficient advantage of the power of the medium. We'll have more later, but just to stimulate your appetite:

- Have you considered sending yourself e-mail as reminders of important projects?

- Do you use e-mail and the Net as a means to research important questions for your company or your family?

- Do you use e-mail to document problems with a supplier?

- Do you make the most of e-mail as a means to keep in touch with friends or family who live hundreds or even thousands of miles away?

- Do you use e-mail to quickly relay information to a large number of people in your company or your family?

- Do you use e-mail to distribute documents to others in your company rather than printing them out and carrying or mailing them to others?

- Do you use e-mail as a means to share your views on important issues and to work for positive changes in government and society?

6. It's ironic that we aren't taught more about something so vital to our lives. The American Obesity Association reports that over 54% of the adult population in the United States is overweight. Most of us did not learn at an early age how destructive it is to consume too much sugar, fat, and starch. Many of us would have benefited significantly from earlier instruction on nutrition and help in establishing healthy diet and exercise habits.

Proficiency with computers is becoming increasingly important, and many children are growing up more skilled with the computer medium than their parents. Most of us, however, have not had instruction in strategies for handling e-mail. The executive quoted at the beginning of this chapter who has his secretary print off his e-mail messages could have benefited from training. And the executive who receives three hundred e-mails a day very much needs effective strategies.

An increasing number of companies and organizations are becoming concerned about the development of e-mail policy, and we have more to say about that in a future chapter. The initial motivations for those policies, however, are likely to be negative. Here are a few common corporate policies which might be affecting you:

- Don't use the company's computers to send personal e-mail. That's misuse of company equipment.

- Don't save old e-mail for so long that it might be used against the company in litigation. E-mail files are rather routinely made subject to subpoena when legal actions are taken against a company. The presence of the e-mail can increase time and expense in responding to the litigation. Don't use e-mail in any way that might harm the company in litigation.

- Don't make threats in e-mail or blow off steam in a way that you wouldn't do through a typed letter or face to face. Such practices increase the danger of litigation.

- Don't fill up your hard disk or the company's servers with e-mail that is no longer needed. That increases the cost of operation for the company and makes it difficult to find needed files.

Making policies, no matter how appropriate or needed, isn't the same as providing people training to properly manage and utilize the power of e-mail. In *E-Mail Rules*, Nancy Flynn and Randolph Kahn estimate that over "81 percent of large employers have written policies governing employee e-mail use. The problem is that fewer than 24 percent of organizations support e-mail policy with employee training" [p. 10]. (And we'll have more to say later about the issue of personal e-mail on company computers. Complete prohibitions of personal e-mail usage tend to create bad will toward the company and encourage employee dishonesty. A slightly less restrictive policy can have some positive results. More about this later!)

7. As with excessive weight gain or loss, it's easy to be in denial about problems with computers in general and with e-mail in particular. Caught up in the rush of activity that is part of life in most companies, schools, other organizations, and homes, we find it easy to ignore problems. We talk about health while shoveling fast food into our mouths and hurrying to the next appointment. We talk about a new running program while driving somewhere in the car. Overall, most of us overeat and underexercise—but we don't do much except talk about it until our clothes start to feel tight or our doctor gives us an unfavorable report on our health.

Many of us rush through the workday answering phone calls, going to meetings, responding to e-mail messages, generating new e-mail, and hurrying home at the end of a too-long day without enough checkmarks on our "to do" lists. We feel too busy to get organized or to think about ways that we might do our work more efficiently. The sheer volume of e-mail has taken many of us by surprise, and we haven't thought about the positive or the negative impact that it has on us.

8.   As is the case with food, there are things that taste great and are enjoyable that may not necessarily be good for us. There is an addictive quality to e-mail and to surfing the Net. Instant messaging is in some respects a wonderful variation of e-mail and the Net. You can have a real-time exchange of typed messages with someone else who is on the Net. Those kinds of exchanges, however, can become addictive and may well take you away from other things you should be accomplishing.

As e-mail becomes increasingly available through small, hand-held devices, it's possible to have a vibration on your belt or in your pocket inform you that you have received e-mail. But what kind of life will you have if you stop what you are doing every single time an e-mail is sent to you? Many of us have experienced annoyance at the interruptions of meetings, movies, and meals that result from someone feeling it is crucial to take a cell phone call in the middle of another activity. E-mail can be just as demanding as a phone call, and some new models combine the two.

Steve joined an electronic mail group, or listserv, for a religious organization to which he belongs. Such groups are common on the

Net and permit participants to receive copies of all the e-mail written by everyone in the group. People share their opinions on various issues and receive responses from others; you can read the results—or contribute to them if you wish. Steve started receiving twenty to ninety pieces of e-mail a day from the group. Some of it was horribly boring, some of it was very interesting, and some of it raised his blood pressure. He found himself with a strong desire to respond to everything except what was boring. And people responded back to his responses. It was fun, it was stimulating, and it also consumed large blocks of time. Those blocks of time could have been spent doing something more productive like working on his part of this book!

Quick Chocolate Oatmeal Cookies

1 stick butter	2 c. white sugar
3 T. cocoa	1/2 c. milk

Boil above ingredients for 1 minute. Remove and mix in the following:

1 tsp. vanilla	1/2 c. peanut butter
1/2 cup coconut	3 c. quick oatmeal

Drop by teaspoon onto waxed paper and cool.

Marilyn Drudge

But what if you aren't having any e-mail problems at all? You aren't too fat; you aren't too thin. Did you waste your money on this book?

Certainly not! (At the very least, you've made a financial contribution to two wonderful households which, in turn, make charitable contributions to worthy causes!)

And the truth is that the absence of diet problems today doesn't guarantee an absence of those problems in the future. You'll learn strategies in this book which will spare you the consequences of creeping e-mail obesity later in life and help you make the most of e-mail now!

Chapter Three
Maintaining Your Diet at Work
Understanding Basic Workplace Issues

- *The first section on "E-Mail at Work" raises some important issues for those who use e-mail in a work setting. If you use e-mail only on a personal basis, then you may want to skip this section and go to page 31.*

- *The second section on "E-Mail Style" covers some basics but also raises important style concerns for anyone using this medium. We want to discourage you from skipping it.*

- *The third section on "Human Nature" raises some issues about the nature of this medium which we feel are important.*

E-Mail at Work

Am I going to get in trouble for sending and receiving personal e-mail at work? In many companies, you can. Some companies have no policy on e-mail; some have very liberal and open policies; and some have very restrictive policies. As a rule of thumb, if you work for a company where supervisors get uptight and turn red in the face because you receive an occasional personal phone call at work, you can be reasonably sure that you won't earn points for receiving and sending electronic mail on the company's computer system during working hours. You may also discover that the administrator of the company's computer system network may actually read some or all of your e-mail.

That's right. Almost certainly some system administrator has the ability (and perhaps the authority) to read your e-mail messages. In one company, a man and woman were terminated from their positions because a system administrator monitored over a thousand pieces of sexually explicit e-mail which they had exchanged. They weren't dismissed because the mail was sexually explicit but because they were doing it on the company's computer system and not doing their work.

Both employers and parents can utilize spy software like eBlaster. This software will secretly forward all e-mail coming into your computer directly to the spy's e-mail. You read your own e-mail, never realizing that a supervisor has received the same message and will also receive your response. This happens even if you are using a private, nonbusiness account through Yahoo or Hotmail. Many employees think they are keeping personal matters private by utilizing a Yahoo or Hotmail account that is separate from their business e-mail, but that doesn't necessarily guarantee privacy when using the company's computer.

> **An important aside:** Parents may find a program like eBlaster a helpful means to know what their children are doing through the computer medium, particularly if there are periods of time when parents are not home and children are using the computer. With many parents concerned about predators on the Net attempting to make contact with their children, it's easy to understand the attractiveness of such programs. But would the same parents spy on the telephone conversations of their children? Balancing protection, trust, and privacy is not always an easy thing to do. Education may prevent more problems than spying.

There are also products like WinWhatWhere that capture every single keystroke a user types at a computer. There are products that take screen shots at particular intervals of everything a computer user does. It's actually very easy for employers to spy on employees. The numbers of employees being supervised and the vast quantity of e-mail and other computer activity provides some protection, although those who are spying also may have software that lets them search for certain key words or phrases. Unless your employer has a clear policy of not monitoring computer activity of employees or at least of not monitoring private e-mail accounts, you should be cautious about what you do on an employer-provided computer system.

E-mail can also result in unexpected legal consequences. Some readers will remember the controversy generated when police officers in California assaulted a black suspect named Rodney King. The fact that the assault was videotaped caused significant problems for the officers at trial. E-mail also made a contribution to the case against the officers. One police officer was confronted with an e-mail message he had written shortly after the assault which read: "Oops, I haven't beaten anyone so bad in a long time."

The authors of this book are not unhappy that the e-mail message helped expose the brutality of the officer. The example, however, clearly shows the danger of making such statements in e-mail. Certain e-mail messages also played a role in the government's lawsuit against Microsoft.

Many of us function under the illusion that e-mail is private. That isn't true. The issues concerning e-mail privacy are still being worked out. One fact that is very clear, however, is that an employer does have the right to monitor what is done on company equipment. Some exercise that right; some do not.

Does that mean your own e-mail sent from your own computer through a service provider you pay is automatically private? Well, not necessarily. Service providers generally include in their service agreements the right to do some monitoring of e-mail. There are universities which monitor e-mail to ensure safe learning environments. If you use sexist or racist language in such settings, you may find your e-mail message being returned to you with a reprimand. If your language is considered hateful or appears intended to cause harm to others, there could be more serious consequences. One major Net service provider screens customer e-mail for profanity. Use too much bad language there, and your e-mail will come back to you. Your service provider may have a readily available link which takes you to their privacy policy, or you may have to e-mail a help desk or an administrator to find out what that policy is.

This doesn't mean you are completely without rights where e-mail is concerned. Unless you explicitly give it up, for example, you retain a copyright to what you have written. That is true even without a copyright notice being included. Your company may have an implied license to copy and utilize whatever you write while at work, but it doesn't automatically have the right to distribute that outside its own e-mail system.

What kinds of issues need to be addressed in e-mail policies? This question is one of increasing importance to companies, educational institutions, government agencies, and other organizations. Some discussion of that belongs in this book because companies as well as individuals can become obese with accumulated e-mail. Here are some of the concerns that e-mail policies should address:

Who owns e-mail produced on company equipment? Most companies and organizations are going to claim that ownership. That's a reasonable claim; and in fact, it would be difficult to conduct business without that ownership.

Does the company have the right to monitor e-mail and other computer activity? Most companies are going to claim that right. Even if the company wants to provide reasonable employee privacy, there are reasons to monitor besides routine "snooping." A company may reasonably want to do studies of volumes of e-mail sent and kinds of e-mail sent. There are issues of server capacity, network capacity, and storage capacity to be considered. A company may also find itself with a legal problem involving an employee which is virtually impossible to handle without monitoring e-mail. When a particular employee is on vacation and a problem comes up concerning a client with whom that employee has been working, it may be crucial for the company to feel free to examine e-mail files of that employee—just as the company would examine paper files from a filing cabinet for needed information.

Can personal e-mail be sent or received? What about personal Net activity of other kinds? Companies are likely to say that company equipment cannot be used for personal purposes. That's a logical position to take, but there are a couple of problems with it. First, does the company want to invest the time, energy, and money to enforce such a policy? If there is no enforcement, then the policy becomes meaningless. If there is enforcement, no matter what the policy says about ownership of e-mail, people will feel that their privacy has been violated and may even be outraged. A company that rigidly enforces such a policy invites lowered employee morale as a consequence. Second, does the company want to encourage employees to be deceitful? If an activity is prohibited but is one that employees are likely to do anyway, then the existence of the policy encourages deceit. Most companies want to nurture an environment in which employees are open and honest. A rigid policy that large numbers will violate works against that kind of atmosphere.

Another approach is to craft a policy that says that the company does not object to minimal levels of personal e-mail but that it reserves the right to monitor such activity and to restrict it if it is, in the opinion of the company, interfering with productivity. This places personal e-mail use in the same category as the way many companies view personal telephone calls—the company recognizes that some such calls are inevitable, that they represent a convenience to employees, and that it is healthier to be open about such calls than deceitful. An employee who does not have (and perhaps cannot afford) a home computer system and e-mail service will find the ability to receive and send small amounts of personal e-mail a significant fringe benefit and may have higher morale as a result. As with phone use, however, there can be instances in which the company has to say: "You are abusing the privilege and interfering significantly with productivity. Stop it."

An increasing number of companies are formulating privacy policies that include the topic of e-mail. You should ask about such policies, which may cover how the company handles financial information about you and other privacy issues in addition to e-mail. Privacy policies are important in a time in which some firms have placed video systems in restrooms to catch people using illicit drugs. Most employees find that kind of invasiveness completely unacceptable. If that kind of invasive supervision is going to be done, then it's important for employees to be informed of the possibility so that they do not feel betrayed if it happens.

Personal e-mail is one matter; personal surfing of the Net is another! Most companies will want to discourage excessive surfing of the Net for personal purposes on company time. The Net offers marvelous possibilities for getting information on a huge number of topics—many of which are work related. It has the potential, however, to be a black hole which sucks up enormous amounts of time. Many of us need to be reminded of the addictive nature of Net surfing. Steve and Marty have both dropped hours at a time going in quest of one thing on the Net and getting sidetracked by many fascinating websites encountered along the way.

In companies where many employees work far more than forty hours a week and often take significant amounts of work home on evenings and the weekend, it is probably not wise company policy to complain because an employee takes a few minutes at work to search for vacation information on the Net. Policies can be crafted that discourage excessive Net surfing at work but leave open occasional personal searching. Again, this has some similarity to personal use of the company telephone system. It's not wise to adopt too prohibitive a policy and thereby lower morale and encourage deceitfulness. The majority of employees will not abuse the privilege. When someone does, it's better to deal directly with that person than to adopt a rigid policy that will be resented by the vast majority who do not abuse such privileges.

How long are e-mail messages and responses supposed to be saved? Even though electronic storage space is increasingly inexpensive, the more e-mail that is saved, the more difficult it is to find what you need, even with sophisticated search programs.

Companies also have appropriate concerns in this area because of the fact, already briefly shared in this book, that a subpoena can cover e-mail messages. Since e-mail messages are often shorter, more informal, and more quickly composed than a paper memo or letter, they also can make the company more vulnerable. People will (rightly or wrongly!) put things in an e-mail message that they would not put in a printed memorandum or letter. One way to deal with the potential legal implications of that is not to keep old e-mail messages hanging around, bulging the network waistline.

We'll say more about the prompt handling and disposal of e-mail messages in our chapter "How to Develop Lifetime Slenderness." We want to suggest here, however, that a good corporate policy encourages people to make prompt decisions about whether to delete or properly file an e-mail message that has been received or sent. Many companies find it a wise matter of practical policy to automatically delete all e-mail messages which have not been intentionally saved to a designated folder within sixty days. Such a policy carries the risk that important information may be deleted, but it guarantees that disk space will not become unduly cluttered with e-mail which is no longer relevant. One of the safeguards on such automatic deletions is that, as far as internal company e-mail is concerned, there are two people who have opportunity to electronically file important communications: the sender and the recipient. Whether there is any decision about automatic deletion or not, it's important to have a policy which encourages prompt decisions about whether or not e-mail should be saved.

The fact that you delete an e-mail or another file on your computer desktop doesn't automatically guarantee that the message is gone. Some recovery software can still find deleted materials on your disk. Many companies automatically back up all the files on the network at the end of the day. Those back-up copies may be retained for weeks, months, or years, containing the e-mail or other file an employee thought had been deleted. Both the White House and Microsoft have had problems because damaging e-mails were recovered from computer systems. Companies need to think carefully about their back-up policies and about the potential problems of retaining those files for too great a period of time.

Human resources matters like compensation issues and performance evaluations may be better communicated by telephone or by traditional letter than too quickly shared through e-mail. A hastily written e-mail message can come back to provide significant problems.

Some companies are tempted to suggest that important e-mail messages be printed and filed in traditional cabinets. While there certainly will be times when a hard copy of an e-mail message is important, the routine printing of e-mail messages should be discouraged. The practice of printing messages eliminates some of the benefits of the electronic communication and generally costs more in paper, ink, and filing space than keeping the same message in a computer file. The prophecies of becoming a paperless society are yet to be fulfilled. According to government statistics, we use twice as much paper per person now as thirty years ago! We may live in an age with the potential of full electronic banking, but we're actually writing triple the number of checks we did thirty years ago. Some people are paying more bills electronically and direct deposit has become more common for payroll, but we are far from paperless on financial transactions.

Most of us are using more paper than ever, but that's not necessarily good for company finances or for our forests! We'll have more to say later about organizing computer files in ways which let you readily retrieve e-mail messages.

What's to be done about chain letters? Chain letters have hit the Internet and are being distributed in incredible numbers. Many people are annoyed by chain letters, and some persons are offended by them. Chain letters often offer wealth for those who pass them along and threaten dire consequences to those who do not. Some people become stressed by the threats of doom, and for those persons the chain letters are worse than an annoyance. A healthy policy in this regard is not to pass chain letters, of the paper or the electronic kind, on to other persons.

One of the most recurring chain e-mails concerns the false claim that Bill Gates and Microsoft are paying out money to test how far and how rapidly e-mail messages can be spread around the world. The recipient of the message is encouraged to pass it on to as many people as possible and is told that he or she will receive a certain sum of money for every person to whom the message goes. Such hoaxes are sometimes called urban legends, and there are websites devoted to sharing the truth about these communications. Passing along such a preposterous claim is an annoyance to everyone who receives it and doesn't believe it—and an act of cruelty to those who actually believe the claim.

What standards of conduct apply to e-mail communications in the company? These are matters which should be obvious, but sometimes people need reminders because of the extremely informal and potentially anonymous nature of e-mail communications. Most companies will want to insist that:

- There be no anonymous e-mail messages on company electronic communication systems. The source of e-mail should not be hidden.

- The same standards of courtesy which apply to paper communications apply to e-mail. Offensive language has no place.

- There should not be derogatory remarks about an individual or group's ethnic background, gender, physical or mental abilities, sexual orientation, physical attributes, or age.

- Harassment of any kind is strictly prohibited.

Simply having an e-mail policy doesn't guarantee that there won't be problems involving e-mail. Companies increasingly need to consider the provision of workshops and other training opportunities to help employees learn the best ways to handle e-mail and also to help them understand the reasons for company concern about e-mail.

E-Mail Style

What do I need to know about e-mail style? What are some of the important differences between e-mail and printed letters and memoranda? Readers who consider themselves very familiar with e-mail may wish to skip this section. On the other hand, a review might be helpful. Here are some of the basics of evolving e-mail style in the United States and Canada (and much of the international community as well):

E-mail is generally more informal than regular mail. People do not worry as much about correct spelling and grammar. People also tend to be briefer in e-mail communications (though there are, of course, significant exceptions!). Steve received this e-mail message:

> *Hey, Steve, what about lunch Friday? I'm coming through Fort Wayne, probably will get there about noon, have to leave again by 2:30 pm. If you can, where?*

The header had the e-mail address and the name of the sender. Steve hit reply in his America Online program as soon as he read the message. On the screen provided (and already addressed by the program), Steve wrote:

> *Lunch is fine. Needs to be 12:15 pm. Olive Garden on Coliseum. See you then!*

Both of those messages are far more brief and informal than a printed letter or memorandum—the exchange also took less time than a phone conversation would have. If the other person had not been familiar with Fort Wayne, Steve would have needed to provide directions to the Olive Garden; but this brief exchange was adequate. And there's absolutely no reason to save those messages once the time has gone into a calendar.

But not all messages should be quickly composed and informal. Suppose that you're wanting to send the president of your company an idea for a new product or service. Then you don't want to be as informal or quick with your e-mail message as the preceding example. You want to compose the message with great care, perhaps going through two or more "drafts," and you may want to ask the opinions of some other people before sending it, as well as passing it through a spell check in your e-mail software.

E-mail is often spontaneous, but it shouldn't be thoughtless! Don't say something in an e-mail message that you wouldn't put in a printed letter or say over the telephone. Rude is rude. Discourteous is discourteous. Insensitive is insensitive—in e-mail or any other medium.

Respect the confidentiality of other people. E-mail makes it easy to forward a message from one person to another (most e-mail systems provide an electronic button you can click to forward something—then you just insert the address of the person you want to receive it). But remember that people have a right to expect privacy in their communication with you. Request permission before forwarding to someone else, or posting to an electronic bulletin board or mailing list, someone else's e-mail message to you.

Be sensitive to issues of sexism and racism. You can get in trouble for sexist and racist statements over the phone or in printed letters, and you also can get in trouble for them in e-mail. Writing something like: "Maryann sure sounds like a bitch. Why'd they put a woman on our team?" invites huge negative (formal or informal) consequences—especially if a copy of the message ever finds its way back to Maryann or to one of her friends.

Don't use all upper case or all lower case letters. The practice of using all upper case letters in e-mail is sometimes referred to as "shouting." Using all upper case or all lower case letters may save you a couple of seconds in typing time, but it makes the resulting message more difficult to read. Use a mixture of upper case and lower case as you would in a printed letter.

Don't use multiple question marks of exclamation marks. "What were you thinking??????" can be a form of "shouting."

Make your e-mail easy to read. Consider using bullets (•) if you want to list a number of things. If you want to provide the steps to a process and the order is important, number the steps. Don't make paragraphs so long that they are difficult to get through. Put a blank line between paragraphs for clear separation. If your software program makes it possible for you to embed the address of another person or a website that you want to share, then do so. Embedded addresses let the reader access the other person or site just by clicking on the address.

If your e-mail is going to be unusually long and will cover several topics, say that in the first sentence or paragraph so that the recipient knows time will be needed to consider it. People tend to work their way through e-mails very rapidly and generally expect to find only one topic or question in an e-mail. That's not an argument against longer e-mail communications, but give fair warning early in the e-mail. Then the recipient can print it out if helpful or can defer it to another time if under immediate schedule pressure.

Unless your e-mail is going to a person or persons you know have the same Internet service provider and the same software as yourself, be cautious about inserting graphics and photos into the e-mail itself. If a recipient has less sophisticated software than you or simply different software, your neat looking graphic may just appear as garbage on his or her screen. Be sure not to assume that recipients all have the ability to deal with HTML and not just plain text.

Don't attach a file to your e-mail when it isn't necessary. Virtually all e-mail programs make it possible for you to attach a file to your e-mail message. Working with that file, however, requires some effort on the part of the recipient who must download the file and then attempt to open it with the right software package. When you can incorporate information into the e-mail message itself, you generally make it easier for your recipient.

Of course there are times when attaching a file can be a great benefit, especially when working with persons who aren't in the same building or even in the same community. Steve and Marty both attach manuscript and graphic files to e-mail they exchange with each other and with other coworkers. Having compatible software on both ends makes the file exchange much easier! It's pointless, however, to attach a short file when the contents can easily be incorporated into your e-mail message.

The spread of viruses on the Net has caused most of us to be far more cautious about downloading files from others. Suppose someone has sent you a neat graphic, like a jumping reindeer or a dancing baby (both of which were popular on the Net at one period of time). The temptation is to immediately forward that file to friends, family, and coworkers. But what do you really know about the source of the graphic? Your friend wouldn't knowingly send you a file which had a virus attached, but is your friend aware of the producer of the graphic? Downloading files onto your computer opens you to the risk of a computer virus. Be cautious about downloading a file when you don't know the person or organization that created the file — and don't forward such things to other people.

More and more computer users who have digital cameras are attaching photographs to e-mails. That's a wonderful way to use the medium. Remember that some photographs take up considerable file space and require significant time to download, depending on the kind of equipment the recipient has. Another alternative that increasing numbers of people use is that of posting the photographs on a website which others can visit — downloading only pictures that they especially want to keep.

Use spell check. Misspelled words in an e-mail message may not be as negatively received as in a printed letter or memorandum, but they certainly don't make you look smart!

Use emoticons or smileys but don't become sickening with them! Most of us enjoy the emoticons or smileys that are often used in e-mail messages, but too many of them can be annoying. Smileys or emoticons generally follow the punctuation mark at the end of a sentence. Here are some of the most common (all made with standard keyboard keys):

:)	happy
:(	sad
;)	wink

Don't raise questions in e-mail if you don't want responses! Whether sending your electronic mail to an individual or to an entire list of individuals, don't ask a question you don't want answered! People do take e-mail seriously and may devote considerable time to a question you raise. Then they'll send you more e-mail, which doesn't help your weight loss program!

Send a copy to yourself or save a copy of your e-mail if you are likely to want to refer again to what you wrote. Saving the copy to your hard disk or workplace network means that it will be there forever unless you consciously delete it at a future time. Sending yourself a copy and leaving it in your electronic mailbox until you receive the needed response is a way to keep it available for reference without holding onto it when it is no longer needed. Consider this question: Is the purpose of this e-mail more like a phone call or more like a letter or memorandum? If it's more like a phone call, you probably don't need a copy unless you would have made notes about your part of the phone conversation. If it's more like a letter or memorandum, then you may want a copy available. Some e-mail systems like Outlook automatically save a copy of your e-mail in a "sent items" folder.

Human Nature

The Net is the transportation medium for e-mail, but it is also a great deal more than that, for it's filled with websites and other opportunities. Our focus in this small book is on e-mail, but we will also talk about some Net possibilities and concerns. It's difficult for many of us to fully grasp the awesome nature of the Net or the incredible speed with which it has grown.

Some people have compared the Net with television. Certainly that comparison has merit, but the Net is both better and worse than television. Consider some of the similarities and differences:

- To catch a particular television program, you have to be watching at the right time — or you have to record the show for later viewing. Websites, however, are available all of the time.

- Parental control is an issue for both television and the Net. There are some shows that children should not watch, and there are some websites that children should not visit. Many Net service providers make available filters and other safeguards to make it easier for parents to keep their children out of adult-oriented websites.

- Television exposes us to different ways of viewing issues and problems. The Net does the same, but it offers a more interactive approach. Websites, electronic bulletin boards, chat rooms, newsgroups, and other means make it possible to actively participate in debates and in the exchange of ideas.

- Television lets you encounter people you would not otherwise meet through the programs which are offered. The Net vastly expands the numbers of people you can encounter — and it lets you enter into dialogue with them. You can in fact get to know them by entering into e-mail exchanges.

- The Net lets you enter into new relationships that are impossible through the television medium. For the most part, those are wonderful opportunities. You can make new friends or be in contact with people in your same field of work in other parts of the country or the world. You can learn an enormous amount. You can, however, be victimized by people you don't know — who may not actually be whom they appear to be in an electronic chat room or through an electronic bulletin board.

There is an anonymous aspect to communication on the Net when you are exchanging e-mail with people you do not know in any other context. That anonymity sometimes lets people show aspects of their "true selves" that they would not in a face-to-face conversation. People may be more vulnerable and open at times precisely because they are in dialogue with persons they don't know or see on a daily basis. That same anonymity can tempt people to take advantage of others. Don't let fear keep you from reaching out across the electronic highways, but do exercise healthy caution.

In her insightful book *Release 2.0*, Esther Dyson writes: "One of the major points I want to get across is the profundity of the changes that the Net will bring to human *institutions* — and its lack of impact on human *nature*. . . . The Net is not going to push us into some antiseptic, digital landscape. It is a medium for us to extend our intellectual and emotional selves, but it will not change our basic characters" [p. 4].

Most of the e-mail that we send will be to family, friends, and coworkers. The potential for vastly expanding our circle of friends, acquaintances, and coworkers through the Net, however, is enormous. Remember that both for better and for worse — human nature stays pretty much the same! Fortunately the Net overall seems to bring out the best in people.

Unadorned Brownies *(No need for icing)*

2 squares (2 oz.) unsweetened chocolate
1/3 c. shortening   1 c. sugar
2 eggs   1 c. flour
1/2 tsp. baking powder   1/2 tsp. salt
1/2 tsp. broken pecans

Melt chocolate and shortening together over hot water. Beat in sugar and eggs. Sift flour, baking powder, and salt together, and stir into the chocolate mixture. Mix in the broken pecans. Spread in well-greased 9" x 9" pan. Bake until top has a dull crust, 30–35 minutes. A slight imprint will be left when top is touched lightly with finger. Cool slightly; then cut into squares.

Mary Uhrig

Aunt Marge's Candy

Melt in microwave for 1-1/2 to 2 minutes the following:
6 oz. chocolate chips
6 oz. butterscotch chips
2 T. butter

Add:
1-1/2 c. honey roasted peanuts
Drop by spoonfuls on waxed paper to harden.

Dorothy Tripp

Chapter Four
What's Your
Restaurant of Choice?
A Quick Look at Options in Software

In the work environment, many people have little or no choice about the e-mail system they utilize. A particular network and e-mail software are provided for everyone in the company, and using something different would either be against company policy or a complication for those who maintain the computer hardware, software, and network. Some people, however, have the ability to make a conscious choice about the software they will use to prepare, read, and file e-mail.

If you have no choice in the matter and aren't interested in knowing what options are available, then you may wish to skip this chapter and go to the next one, "How to Develop Lifetime Slenderness." Some without a choice themselves may want to skim this chapter simply because it is helpful to know what others are using for e-mail communication. Increasing numbers of people have one combination of software and Internet service provider at their place of work and another at home. Each combination has its own pluses and minuses — and its own e-mail address book!

If you go to McDonald's or Burger King, you aren't likely to find many selections that are good for your heart. Fast food is a great convenience for many of us, but choosing a fast food restaurant limits the other options available. You may have some lower fat options at Subway, but if your taste buds are set on a hamburger and fries, you'll be disappointed. In a similar way, your selection of software controls some of your e-mail options. The good news is that there are a lot of fairly good software products for work with e-mail.

From our point of view as authors, this is the most frustrating chapter in the book to write. The analogy between e-mail software (used to create, read, and file the e-mail messages that get sent) and restaurants is a little too close to reality! People who review restaurants for a living are frequently frustrated when they release their opinions in book form because:

- Some restaurants they recommend are out of business by the time the book is in print.

- Some excellent new restaurants open, and readers are disappointed to find nothing written about them.

- Many restaurants make frequent menu changes with the result that the descriptions in the book aren't always accurate.

- Sometimes the restaurant changes the head chef with the result that things get a lot better or a lot worse than at the time the book was written.

There's nothing we can do to change the fact that some of this information will be wrong by the time the book is in print. For further updates, we suggest you visit our website, which can be found at www.emaildietbook.com. Another good source of current information is the The Open Group Electronic Messaging Association (EMA) Forum, www.opengroup.org/messaging/.

E-Mail Software

Many people will simply handle their e-mail using the software that is available through their Internet service provider. Providers like AOL, Yahoo, and MSN make it easy to send e-mails, attach files, and attach photographs. They can check your spelling if you want and have conveniently integrated address books. Gmail, the e-mail service from Google, which is currently being tested, offers generous e-mail storage and an excellent search engine for retrieving e-mail. You can, however, get a separate e-mail software program that will give you more options in how you handle e-mail than you can get through any of these service providers.

Eudora set the standard for e-mail software for some time. You can use Eudora with any Internet service provider. It was named for author Eudora Welty who wrote a story called "Why I Live at the P.O." A free version of Eudora is available (through the Net at www.eudora.com), but that version doesn't give all the very attractive bells and whistles of Eudora Mail Pro, which can be purchased for a reasonable price. This is excellent software, which has sophisticated filters (that can help you control the flow of junk e-mail). It also uses VirusScan to check the e-mail you receive for viruses (though viruses are more likely to be in an attached file rather than in the e-mail itself).

Eudora Mail Pro also connects well with encryption options from other suppliers. Businesses or individuals who send e-mail of a highly confidential nature may find it attractive to protect their e-mail from others with an encryption (coding) program. Many "switches" make it possible for you to customize Eudora to do things for you like checking for your mail automatically at predetermined time intervals. If you are looking for features beyond the e-mail handling capability of your service provider, you won't go wrong with Eudora.

If you use a software program like Eudora, you'll want to consider *popping* your mail from the Internet service provider directly onto your computer. This allows you to automatically save and organize your e-mail in a variety of ways, taking advantage of the power of the software. Your Internet service provider may have a limit on how many e-mail messages can be stored, whereas the limit on your own computer is the available space on your hard drive. If you use more than one computer, however, you want to be careful where you pop your mail. You could end up with e-mail distributed across several machines.

Microsoft Outlook Express is a very powerful communication program that lets you work with e-mail and newsgroups. Newsgroups (sometimes called listservs) are groups of people who exchange e-mails on topics of mutual interest. Belonging to a newsgroup can provide you with lots of useful information and also with LOTS of e-mail.

If you have multiple e-mail and newsgroup accounts, you can work with them all through one window by using Outlook Express. You can arrange to have e-mails from your work service provider and your home service provider automatically appear in Outlook Express in a way similar to Eudora Pro. You can also create multiple e-mail identities for yourself if you want to keep separate, for example, your work and your personal e-mail. AOL, unfortunately, has a protocol that makes it very difficult to get e-mail downloaded to Outlook Express (at least as of this date).

Outlook Express has a very good address book feature and will save names and addresses automatically (if you want) as you reply to messages. It's also easy to import names and addresses from most other programs and service providers into Outlook Express.

Outlook Express lets you use a system of "rules" to help you handle large volumes of e-mail. The rules let you sort incoming messages into different folders, highlight certain messages in color, automatically reply to or forward certain messages, and much more. Outlook Express also offers a helpful calendar function.

Both Eudora Pro and Outlook Express are powerful tools to help handle e-mail. Kaitlin Duck Sherwood has written a very helpful book called *Overcome Email Overload with Microsoft Outlook*. Taking advantage of these programs, however, requires that you commit some time to studying how they work—like the time to read Sherwood's book, which is considerably longer than this one! Multiple folders and rules for sorting incoming mail work well for some people but can be confusing for others. If you buy one of these programs, be sure to make the investment in time to study it and get the most out of it. But also see what you can learn from the strategies we'll be sharing in the book you are holding in your hand right now.

Lotus Notes is a database and communications program which many large businesses are utilizing. Lotus Notes gives you very sophisticated features for handling e-mail and also makes it relatively easy for many people to share and contribute to databases of information. It has a calendaring and scheduling feature. This is powerful software, and, as with Eudora Pro and Outlook Express, it takes time to learn how to get the most from it. If your company provides it, rejoice and invest the time to learn how to use it. You'll be pleased with the result, and properly used it will almost inevitably become more and more essential to communication within your organization.

Chandler is a new product known as a Personal Information Manager (PIM). It integrates e-mail, an appointment calendar, and a contact list in creative ways. Chandler is code-named for the detective novelist Raymond Chandler and is being developed by the Open Source Application Foundation with the involvement of Mitch Kapor. It's designed for ease of personal use and to make it easy to share information with others. We're sure you will be hearing more about it in the months ahead. It could be a good alternative to Lotus Notes, especially for small organizations and for personal use.

There are many other software options, most of which are relatively good. We know many people who have purchased bundled computer systems who are delighted with the e-mail software which is included. We also know many who have an e-mail software package sitting on their hard disk but who elect simply to use the e-mail management tools which are provided by their ISP.

What Do We Recommend?

The answer, as you've already gathered, is that "it depends." If you have an ISP and a software program provided through your company or other organization, then obviously that's your foundation for work with e-mail. In some organizations, you may still have the option of choosing a software program to make your handling of e-mail more efficient. Our bias would be to go with Eudora Pro or Outlook Express, though those are only two of many fine options.

Lotus Notes, as already shared, can be very powerful software for a business or other organization. It's not very useful for only one or two people to have Lotus Notes. The advantage comes when most of the people with whom you interact have the software. If your company isn't currently using Lotus Notes and if the exchange of information is very crucial to your success, encourage those who do decision making to take a close look at the Lotus Notes option.

If you are making decisions for a small business or for your own home, our recommendation would be that you initially go with a major ISP such as America Online, Yahoo, or MSN and utilize the e-mail handling capabilities that are made available by that provider. The ease of connecting to the Net and the ease of use of the e-mail software will make the whole process much less intimidating. As you gain comfort and experience, you can consider changes. You might want later to change to a less expensive connection to the Net. You might want to go with a more powerful e-mail handling option such as Eudora or Outlook Express. For many small businesses and individuals, the capabilities from a major ISP will meet your needs for a substantial period of time—and will not require a lengthy learning curve.

Some of you reading this book have substantial knowledge and experience with computers and with the Net. If you are in that category of sophisticated users, you probably already have your own preferences on ISPs and on e-mail handling software. We'd be interested in hearing what works well for you and why you like it.

Why are you including chocolate recipes in a book that has dieting in the title? Well, that's a good question. First, because we have the recipes, and we think they are good! Second, because the key to good health is not just losing weight but having a healthy balance in the food consumed. To us, it seems like chocolate ought to be part of that balance! We all know that chocolate has more than a few calories and fat grams, but it's not without health benefits! For example:

- Some new research suggests that cocoa flavanols may inhibit platelet formation in a way similar to the beneficial effect of low dose aspirin. 2002 and 2003 research suggests that chocolate may improve blood vessel function.
- The cocoa bean is the richest source of magnesium in nature, and magnesium deficiency is linked to heart disease.
- Rich, dark chocolate contains iron, calcium, and vitamins A, B1, C, D, and E.
- Chocolate does have some antioxidant value and may be a help in preventing cancer (though we don't know how much help!). The richer and darker the chocolate, the higher the antioxidant value.

Chapter Five
How to Develop
Lifetime Slenderness
Identifying Some Basic Principles
for Keeping Fit

DON'T SKIP THIS CHAPTER! This chapter is in many ways the core of the book. If you aren't going to read any other chapter, read this one. If you are glancing through this book in a bookstore, THIS is the chapter to read.

E-mail has a great deal in common with potato chips, taco chips, and popcorn. It's almost impossible to have just one! There's really no point in opening a bag of potato chips if you should only eat four or five of them. Who wants just a taste? But the whole bag? That probably isn't good for you. E-mail can be wonderful, fun, and delicious. But just as too many bags of potato chips can cause the extra pounds to stick to your tummy, thighs, or hips, too many e-mails can block your productivity and raise your anxiety.

No business, church, community service organization, government agency, college or university, or household functions well without a great deal of communication. That communication comes in many forms including:

- Phone calls (regular and cellular)
- Voice mail (regular and cellular)
- Letters
- E-mails
- Instant messaging (IM)
- Fax documents
- Pager messages
- Interoffice print memos
- Newsletters
- Scheduled appointments
- Drop-in visits
- Meetings
- Conferences (live and video)

Some communications are necessary and vital to the work of the business, organization, or household. Some of them are necessary but take considerably more time than needed. Some of them are necessary but come at inconvenient times — making it more difficult to get work accomplished. And some of them are completely unnecessary, which means they are inconvenient no matter when they come.

As we've already discussed, the amount of communication that happens by e-mail continues to increase — at an extraordinarily high rate in many organizations. E-mail has the potential to be more efficient and more convenient than many other kinds of communication. You can read and respond to it when you want, and the response mechanism is relatively easy. But the potential volume of e-mail and the difficulty of sorting out what is important from what is unimportant can make the medium seem more like a curse than a blessing.

Work environments can be very stressful. It feels to many of us as though there aren't enough hours in the day to meet all the demands placed upon us. When you already feel overwhelmed and then see 80 e-mails in your box, it's easy to become anxious. We need to find the best ways to handle e-mail not only for efficiency but also for emotional health.

We want to offer you strategies that can help you handle e-mail in ways that increase its convenience and helpfulness rather than adding pounds to the waistline of your e-mail in box and taking too many hours from your busy day. Consider the following:

1. Study your current consumption patterns. This is the place in a good diet book where the authors suggest that you keep track of everything you eat for one or two weeks so that you can better identify the changes you need to make for continuing weight loss. If you only send and receive an average of three or four e-mail messages a day, then keeping track of your e-mail for a week may be realistic. If you send and receive dozens of e-mail messages a day, then monitoring usage for a week will make you crazy! In that event, choose a reasonably typical eight-hour day and record your e-mail consumption for that period of time. If you aren't yet using e-mail, then obviously you aren't going to have any to log; you may want to refer to this section again at a future time when you are making use of the medium. Put a piece of paper on your desk near the computer, and make slash marks as you send and receive e-mail. Although you might decide to use more detailed categories than these, we suggest a very simple chart:

Category	E-mails received	E-mails sent
Work-info		
Work-response		
Work-useless		
Personal		
Personal-useless		
E-mail newsletters or listservs		
Spam or Phishing		

Work-info refers to e-mails in which others are sharing with you information they think you need to have about business concerns — or e-mails you are sending to keep others informed. No response is necessarily expected to these e-mails.

Work-response refers, of course, to business e-mails to which a response is expected.

Work-useless refers to business e-mail that did not give you information that is of any use to you and does not need (or should not need) a response. In other words, there is no good reason for it to have been sent to you. Hopefully you aren't sending others mail in this category — but be honest in your tabulating!

Personal refers to e-mails that are to or from friends, family, or personal business associates (like your stockbroker, banker, or insurance agent).

Personal-useless refers to personal e-mail that is not helpful to you and that you did not particularly want to receive. Again, you are hopefully not sending e-mail like this to others, but. . . .

E-mail newsletters or listservs refers to e-mail you receive from businesses, other organizations, or individuals as a result of your membership in a group, or your subscription to newsletters or e-mail updates. It also refers to messages you receive from newsgroups or listservs.

Spam refers to any e-mail that comes from someone you do not know and is attempting to sell something or persuade you to do something in which you have absolutely no interest. You are likely one of thousands or even millions of people to receive this spam. **Phishing** is an e-mail request for your bank or credit card account information or your identity, such as your place of birth or your mother's maiden name. If you are spamming or phishing yourself, then put this book down, go outside, and lie down in front of an oncoming vehicle.

When you've monitored your e-mail for a day or a week, you'll have a much better idea what the volume is that you are receiving and how much of it is not useful. The suggestions in this chapter can help you take control.

2. **Change your thinking about e-mail and the computer medium.** People who are successful with diets change their thinking about food and fitness. People who go on the South Beach Diet, for example, come to see carbohydrates in a completely different way and take dramatic steps to lower their consumption of them. If you are

going to gain control over e-mail, you need to change your thinking as well. Determine that you are going to make the most of the e-mail medium and enjoy the tastes, but that you aren't going to let it control you.

We'll be making some suggestions that may at first seem uncomfortable to you. For example, we'll be advising that you not answer every e-mail you receive, because not all e-mail needs or deserves a response. We'll also be telling you not to read every e-mail the second you receive it, because that gives e-mail too much control over your schedule. If you've been using e-mail for several months or years, some of those suggestions will seem contrary to the way you've learned to view e-mail. If you really want to gain control of e-mail and make the most of the medium, however, you need to take a fresh look at e-mail practices.

We don't promise that you'll want to implement every suggestion that we offer, and we readily acknowledge that a few suggestions may seem contradictory—because the needs of one person are not necessarily the needs of another. But if you read with an open mind, we do promise there will be strategies here that will help you.

3. Control mailing lists (listservs or newsgroups). People on successful weight loss programs don't leave open boxes of chocolate where they'll be seen throughout the day. They generally avoid stocking high-fat, high-calorie foods in the refrigerator where those options will represent a strong temptation each time the door is opened. Here's some equivalent counsel concerning e-mail:

- Only join a mailing list or newsgroup after careful thought. These groups may offer great entertainment and are often good sources of information. They can also fill up your electronic mailbox in a hurry. As already shared, when you join a group, you receive information on how to get out. Put all such information in a single folder marked "Escape!" so that you know where to find it. Send yourself an e-mail as a reminder to evaluate the list or group in a month; that's usually long enough to get a feel for it. You may also want to unsubscribe from such lists when you are going to be gone for an extended period of time. Some e-mail groups and lists have a feature which permits you to temporarily stop and then start again.

• Some mailing lists or newsgroups have an archive of e-mail exchanges, which let you read the material from a day, a week or a month at one time—rather than having that material added to your electronic mailbox as it is sent. Others may have the e-mails available on a website where you can read them when and if you want to do so.

• If you have a software program like Eudora Pro or Outlook Express, use filters or rules for automatic delivery of these e-mails to a folder or box for e-mails from newsgroups or listservs. Then you can read these at your convenience.

• If you never (or rarely) read e-mails from newsgroups or listservs, unsubscribe now.

• If you find that your electronic mailbox fills up in a hurry, you may want to reevaluate the mailing lists and newsgroups in which you already participate. The fact that such a list or group was valuable once doesn't mean that you continue to receive the same value. Be selective, and ask to be deleted when a group no longer meets an important need or provides you with new information.

4. Think BEFORE giving out your e-mail address. Remember that you don't give out your home address and phone number without thought. Sharing your e-mail address should be no different. If your life is already full, don't get pulled into e-mail correspondence that doesn't advance you professionally or meet important personal needs.

Many organizations put e-mail addresses on letterhead and business cards, and that's an appropriate thing to do in today's technological society. You'll also find, however, that growing numbers of companies, stores, websites, and others ask for your e-mail address. Don't be too quick to share that address. When you do, you open yourself up to all kinds of unsolicited requests and offers. And these organizations share e-mail addresses with others.

When you purchase a new hot water heater, furnace, automobile, or computer, you may be asked for your e-mail address on the warranty card. Think carefully about what actual benefit you gain from the company having your e-mail address rather than just your regular mailing address. **And if they have a box to check offering to send you information on the products of their "partners" (which basically means anyone who pays them money for their e-mail list), leave that box blank.**

The most reputable commercial groups that send out regular e-mail when you register for their products (like Apple or Microsoft) always include a message on how to stop receiving that information. Some groups will give you the option of whether or not your e-mail name and address are shared with others. Unfortunately, many companies will sell your e-mail address without your permission (just as postal mail order companies do with your postal mailing address).

> *Though the issues involved go beyond the scope of this book, you should be aware, if you are not already, that companies are increasingly seeking to do what is often called "database marketing." That means they are seeking not only your name and postal or e-mail address but also as much additional information about you as possible. They put that information into huge databases and then use it for more effective marketing. Some refer to this process as "data mining."*

> *Try doing a search of YOUR e-mail address using Google or another search engine. You may be surprised how many places your e-mail address appears.*

> *When you fill out a survey as part of the registration process for a new product like a computer or a vacuum cleaner, that information often becomes part of a database.*

The information is used for the company's own marketing purposes and is often sold to others. Thus you want to think carefully before too quickly giving out personal information in response to registration forms which claim to want to know more about you to serve you better.

Consider the possibility of having a business e-mail address, a personal e-mail address, and a junk or alternative e-mail address. Deliberately give your own junk e-mail address to organizations likely to sell the address to others. That lets you give an e-mail address to companies from which you purchase products without having your business or personal e-mail address flooded with spam.

5. Enlist your friends in the process. Any good diet book reminds you that the support and encouragement of others can make it easier to lose weight. In the case of e-mail, there are a few pragmatic things your friends can do to help you:

- If you don't want to receive frivolous e-mail from friends and business associates, then tell them so. Some people think it's great fun to send jokes, recipes, essays, and other items to their friends via e-mail. Those things may be great fun, but they may also be causing your electronic mailbox to bulge at the seams. You may want to ask people to send such items to you at your home or alternateive e-mail address rather than your business e-mail address.

- Tell your friends at work and in your personal life that you are attempting to get better control of your e-mail. Ask them to give you feedback if they notice that you are unnecessarily responding to e-mail that they send. Do you write back more often than is necessary? Do you send more information than is necessary? When they receive e-mail from you, do they think: "Good, you always have something interesting to share"? OR do they think "Oh, here's another time-waster"? What strategies have they found effective themselves?

- As you talk to your friends at work and in your personal life, you may find that many of them are also having difficulty handling the volume of e-mail they receive. You may be able to help each other and develop stronger will-power as a team than you would as individuals. You can also share strategies.

- Urge your friends to make maximum use of the subject line so that you don't inadvertently delete their mail! You may have difficulty anticipating every possible sender from whom you might genuinely like to hear. Some people have e-mail names which have little or no relationship to their real names. When sorting your e-mail in a hurry, you could inadvertently delete a message from a good friend, whose e-mail name is simply not familiar to you. Some people have a tendency to leave the subject line blank, but it is a good opportunity to immediately give the recipient information about the e-mail and the sender. E-mails with subject lines like these aren't likely to be accidentally deleted:

"Dinner Friday?"
"Beth in the hospital"
"Happy Birthday!"

You may occasionally, inadvertently, delete e-mail from a friend or business associate. When you find out that has happened, simply apologize and explain why it happened.

6. **Reshape your eating/e-mailing style and set new priorities— don't feel that you must immediately read every single e-mail you receive.** Many business and educational networks inform you the moment you receive an e-mail message. The same may be true in your home if your connection to the Internet is through cable or DSL. It's tempting (but generally unwise) to go into your e-mail as soon as you receive such a notification. Determine at what times you are going to read e-mail each day, and then don't let the appearance of an e-mail message distract you from other priorities. Remember that you have far greater flexibility with e-mail than with telephone calls or

53

drop-in visitors. That's one of the best reasons for extensive use of e-mail. You can read when you want and respond when you want.

Telephone calls are frequent interrupters of work, and some people have begun making more extensive use of voice mail to avoid breaks in concentration during work on a major project or while in a discussion with another person. The voice mail message can be received and responded to at a more convenient time. In some instances, the response ends up getting made through the other person's voice mail, and most people are beginning to recognize this as part of business in our time. Caller ID also offers some helpful protection.

Some people, however, have a strong compulsion to answer the phone when it rings even if in the middle of a major project which requires concentration or in the middle of an important meeting with another person. There are some professions and businesses in which that kind of immediate response to the telephone is important, but that's not the case for most of us. The wise use of voice mail generally increases productivity and respects the time of those with whom one is having a face-to-face meeting. For most of us, the desire to answer the phone immediately each time it rings is like a food addiction when one feels a compulsion to eat every time something brings a reminder of food.

E-mail addiction can be like a telephone addiction—in which you begin to believe that you MUST respond immediately to every e-mail you receive. When the "YOU HAVE MAIL" notice begins to flash on the computer screen or the mailbox icon begins to vibrate on the computer desktop, it becomes tempting to immediately leave other work and go read the e-mail. Then the e-mail controls and drives YOU. If your system permits it, you may even wish to have the "YOU HAVE MAIL" notice or the notification sound turned off.

Marty is a college professor, and taught one particular class whose members decided that e-mail was the best possible way to communicate with him and to make a good impression on him. He discovered that in his efforts to respond to the e-mail, work for other projects and classes was piling up, and his quick responses made students think that all requests would be responded to immediately.

It's usually best to read e-mail at just a few set times each day. Many people like the pattern of checking e-mail early in the day, at mid-morning, at noon, and at the end of the day. If you don't receive a lot of e-mail, then once or twice a day may be sufficient. We recommend that you avoid checking your e-mail at the very beginning of the day (unless, of course, you're waiting for an important message). Beginning with e-mail may lead to an hour or more of reading and writing messages, postponing work on more important goals for the day. *Ask yourself: Is reading and responding to e-mail the most important thing that I have to do today? The answer is usually "No."*

E-mail messages often go to multiple persons asking for their feedback or opinions on a particular issue. Being the first to respond on some questions to some people may make you look good. If the president of your company wants input quickly, then there may be points to gain by being among the first to respond. On some issues, however, it's not unusual for twenty-five respondents to share the same two ideas in just slightly different ways. In those instances, the time to compose a response may be a waste for you, and the person reading your response will not feel you've made any original contribution. If someone else has already said what needs to be said and said it well, there may be no need to respond at all — or your response might take the form: "Maria said it well. Thanks!" Or "Kevin has already given my response. Thanks!" Reading your e-mail perhaps three or four times a day keeps you from being too late responding to important requests for information but also gives you opportunity to see how others are responding. You may save time on your response — or reading what others have said may stimulate a more original thought which you can share.

When you read an e-mail message, immediately ask yourself what you need to do in response to the message. Suggestion seven, on the next page, gives more specific counsel on this. The point here is not to delay. It's best to read your e-mail at times when you can spare a few minutes to respond to the most important or time-sensitive messages. Many e-mails can be answered in two minutes or less.

You may work in an organization where immediate response to all e-mail messages is expected. If that's the case, then you obviously have to conform to that expectation. You might want, however, to pass a copy of this book to the person responsible for such policies or expectations. Requiring people to respond with the same immediacy to e-mail as to telephone calls misses much of the strength of the e-mail medium. If something really needs to be shared or asked immediately, then that should be done with a telephone call rather than with an e-mail. Voice mail should be checked more frequently than e-mail in most organizations. Much of the power of e-mail comes in the ability to read and to send when it's convenient to do so and to give adequate thought to the messages read and sent.

An exception to this counsel comes for persons who work in a customer service department. Immediate responses to requests for information or orders ARE the priority of many people in customer service positions.

Caution: Be very careful about using the option with your service provider or software program which automatically retrieves e-mail for you at specified intervals. Be sure that you don't specify automatic downloading of files which are attached to e-mail messages. Viruses can be spread through attached files. You don't want to download files unless you know the person sending the files and have confidence in that person's judgment in matters of computer technology. Many well-intentioned people pass along files of dancing babies, talking dogs, and other interesting graphics which they think you'll appreciate. The sender may not be aware that a virus is attached to the file. With more sophisticated viruses beginning to appear in the text of e-mails as well as in attached files, caution is also appropriate in opening e-mail messages.

7. **The old adage for handling paper said: "Handle each piece of paper only one time."** Well, that actually never did work. One letter or e-mail received may require two days of work or thought for response; you can't necessarily neglect everything else to immediately answer that kind of message no matter what medium it comes through. Many e-mail messages, however, can be answered in as little as thirty seconds. Others waste your reading time completely! Here are some **Stress-Free Strategies** to help you move through your e-mail quickly. Make an immediate decision with each e-mail:

- **Read it or delete it!** If you do not know the sender and the subject line obviously looks like spam, then don't bother reading it. If this strategy makes you too uneasy, then use a filter or a rule in a program like Eudora Pro or Outlook Express to put such e-mail in a folder for future review. Doing that, however, only delays the decision to delete. If the subject line is offering you Viagra, a cure for baldness, credit repair, or "see my sexy pictures," you have little to lose by deleting the e-mail without reading it.

  Some e-mail software programs have a "delete" folder or trash can in which messages you mark "delete" are placed. Then you still have to go back to that folder at a future time and clear it out. Going back to the same messages is a waste of time. Make your decision when you first read it, and be done with it. If you can't keep yourself from using this feature, then at least set it up so that the mail in the "delete" folder is automatically deleted after a certain amount of time.

- **Respond immediately and then delete the message** unless your system will do an automatic deletion after a certain period of time. When making the decision to delete, try thinking about the e-mail as a telephone call. Would you type up a set of minutes or record and transcribe the same exchange if it had been over the telephone? As a default, we have a tendency to keep things which come to us on paper, and we tend to keep too much. While some e-mail messages are like letters sent through the postal service and need to be saved, many are more similar to what would be handled by a phone call. Keep those e-mail calories back; when in doubt, delete! (With some software and some network systems, automatic deletion can be customized to the period of time you or the network administrator selects.)

- **Respond immediately, and save the e-mail and your response.** If the e-mail is one you may wish to look at again, save it in an appropriate folder by project or date. You may occasionally receive e-mail that has contractual or other legal implications, which means you should save it even though you will probably not want to read it again. Be sure of your company's policies about such things.

- **Read the message, and determine that no response is needed.** If the sender indicates that it is strictly "For Your Information" (FYI), don't complicate it by responding unnecessarily. Doing that can set in motion a series of unneeded e-mails. For example, consider this series of e-mail exchanges:

From Betty to Steve: Just wanted you to know that the article you sent is exactly what we wanted, and we'll print it in the June issue. You'll receive a check within a month, and your endorsement of the check constitutes acceptance of the terms I sent you earlier.

From Steve to Betty: Thanks! I didn't know that I actually got paid for doing the article. The publicity value of having my name on it was motivation enough.

From Betty to Steve: If I'd known that before, I wouldn't have told you I was sending a check! Just kidding - :):) But seriously, we were on such a tight budget for a non-profit publication that we used to never pay for articles. Now we have a little more to work with and feel like offering some payment makes people more willing to write again. I guess I didn't tell you the exact amount, which is $200 for an article of that length. Do you think that's enough?

And as you would suspect, that wasn't the end of the e-mail exchange. There were in fact another two e-mails from Steve to Betty and Betty to Steve. If Steve hadn't responded to the first e-mail and had just saved it to a file for reference in case the check didn't arrive, he and Betty would have been spared the other e-mails. Another option would have been for him to have stopped after the first word of his first response: *Thanks!*

Of course there is the possibility that the series of messages was helpful for Betty in thinking about the payment policy, but it wasn't a very pressing issue for Steve, who only wrote one article and didn't anticipate writing any more for that particular publication.

We can help others by clearly indicating when an e-mail message is FYI, and we should encourage them to do the same in their correspondence to us.

After you determine that no response is needed, you still have to determine whether or not to save the message.

- **Forward the message** to another person who is in a better position to respond to it. Sometimes the purpose of an e-mail to you will be to request that you make a connection with someone else, and simply forwarding the e-mail to that individual is the appropriate response.

You want to be careful, however, about forwarding something if the sender doesn't already have the expectation that you may do so. Remember that people have the expectation that they are the owners of what they write. That may not always be the case in the business setting, but people will sometimes respond negatively to automatic forwarding of e-mail. If you are in doubt, then send a quick e-mail back asking for permission. (And don't share someone else's e-mail address unless you are sure it would be all right with that person. Use the same discretion that you would on giving out someone's home address or phone number.)

- **Put the message in a computer file folder for weekly or monthly review,** and have a set time when you do that each week or month. Try not to put things in such a folder unless you absolutely do not have time to respond at the time of reading the message and aren't prepared to schedule a specific block of time to work on a response. If you are getting ready to leave the office for a meeting and find that you have fifteen e-mail messages, you may have no alternative. Respond immediately to the three most pressing and put the other twelve in the weekly review folder (or save them for the next day). Or consider marking as "unread" those messages to which you didn't have time to respond.

- **Save the message AND block off time on your calendar when you are going to do the work required for the response. Do this only when the request is going to require a substantial amount of time to respond. Don't delay scheduling that time, and consider sending yourself an e-mail for delivery on the day you are going to do it (as a reminder).**

- **Delete the e-mail, but first send a response requesting that you be removed from the list.** Take this step when the e-mail message was unsolicited and comes from a source from which you are not interested in receiving future communications. There is a danger in this, however. Some spammers generate potential e-mail addresses and send a barrage of mail to those addresses. Not all the addresses are valid. When they receive a response from such an e-mail, they know that they have a valid e-mail address. They may go right ahead sending you further e-mail. It's often best to simply delete the e-mail rather than to confirm that the address is valid.

- **Forward offensive e-mail to your Internet service provider.** Many service providers have a specific address to which you can forward offensive e-mail. If your provider does not offer that service, then forward it to the technical support or HELP people for the provider. If you make offensive mail an inconvenience to the service provider, then those folks are more likely to try to take corrective action. And they are powerless to act if not informed that you are receiving e-mail that is not only unwanted but actually offensive.

Here's a summary, which also appears on a card included with the book:

Stress-Free Strategies

READ IT OR DELETE IT

If you READ IT, then choose ONE
of the following:

Respond and Delete

Respond and Save

Save or Delete Only

Forward

Put in Weekly/Monthly Folder

Schedule Time

Delete & List Remove

Forward to ISP

---

8. Simply save all of your e-mail except for spam, and rely on the search capabilities of your software to find the e-mails you need. With increasingly sophisticated e-mail software becoming available and hard disk space so inexpensive, you may want to consider this as an alternative to a careful organizational system. It certainly requires less thought as you move through the e-mails you receive.

We are inclined to feel that you will gain from a reasonable organizational system with your e-mail and from deleting those e-mails that have no continuing value. Saving e-mails to the relevant project folders seems especially important because it results in your having everything you need for that task in the same place. If you don't remember that you have an e-mail on a particular topic, your search capabilities won't be of help to you. That brings us to the next strategy. . . .

9. Develop a consistent e-mail filing system. Most of us haven't really thought about the way in which we save e-mail. Some service providers and software programmers make it relatively easy to save e-mail—some will save it forever unless you give a specific delete instruction!

Saving e-mails is, fortunately, not the same as saving pieces of paper because of the convenience of search features on our computers. Because of this, you can use broad categories for the e-mails that you decide to save, making your decision time faster and easier. You do not, for example, need to have a separate folder for correspondence from each person with whom you work. The sophistication of search programs in e-mail software and other computer software continues to increase. Some e-mail software permits you to sort your in box according to sender, subject, date, or priority.

Consider the possibility of saving much of your e-mail in the regular folders you use to organize everything else you have on your computer, not in a special e-mail section. Learning how to do this and doing it consistently will make it easier for you to find documents and will increase the efficiency of your work by keeping things related to particular projects in the same place. Both Steve and Marty maintained "E-Mail Diet Book" folders while they were working on this book. E-mails to each other which were important enough to save went into the same folder as other materials and copy for the book. (They did not, however, save the many e-mails about the logistics of getting together to work on the book. Those were like phone calls; no record needed to be kept once the decisions had been made.)

Some e-mail software, such as Eudora, makes it especially easy for you to direct e-mail into folders and sub-folders; but YOU still have to make the decision about the folders you need and where they are kept. Steve routinely saves e-mails to the folders related to particular projects on which he is working. He keeps e-mails that are not project related (but are still worth saving) in a "correspondence" folder. Marty keeps most of his e-mails that are not project related in an "in box" and at the end of the month moves things into one of six folders he's named for the months of the year: 2006:01–02; 2006:03–04, 2006:05–06, etc. His "in box" contains only messages from the current month.

When you send e-mail to others, use some consistency in what you type as the subject. It should be something that will make sense to you and the other person if either of you is looking at a list of sent or received e-mails two months in the future.

Resist the temptation to print all your e-mail messages and file them in paper folders in filing cabinets. While we are certainly a long way from having a paperless society, printing all the e-mail you send and receive will cause you enormous weight gain in accumulated paper. That would be a little like switching to a "chocolate pie diet" because you aren't sure how many calories you're consuming on your current diet. At least, the reasoning goes, you'll know how many calories you eat if you only eat one thing. You'll know how many calories you consume if you print all your e-mail, and you'll grow to the size of a beached whale! **Don't do it.**

10. Figure out how much "neatness counts" in your company or organization. As suggested in an earlier chapter, in most organizations, e-mail can be done without the amount of concern over grammar, spelling, and punctuation that one has with a printed letter or memo. You can be more informal and less anxious about format, which may save you time; but don't get too sloppy! Those who especially like OR dislike the taste of your e-mail may keep it around for a long time. And never send out e-mail or anything else without running a spell check program—it won't catch everything, but it will catch some errors for most of us.

11. Never respond to an e-mail when you are angry or upset. A good dieting book reminds you of the danger of eating when you are angry or depressed or otherwise emotionally upset—people who do so inevitably eat too much. The same is true for e-mail—people who do so inevitably say too much or may be misunderstood. As important as it is to learn the skill of making quick decisions about how to handle e-mail messages, responding to something when you are angry or upset is never a wise strategy.

Reflecting anger in an e-mail message is commonly known as "flaming" in Net circles, and people always resent it. Like an angry printed letter, an angry electronic letter can continue to hang around for months or years and may be used against you in unlikely situations. While delaying a response in order to cool off may clutter your mailbox or file folders, it will help you avoid the series of correspondence or personal conversations required to make peace later.

12. Recognize that while they probably should not, people will often say things in e-mail that they won't in printed mail. The process of producing printed mail takes longer and gives more time for thought. So when someone sends you a flaming piece of e-mail, don't take offense too quickly and don't escalate the conflict by responding in the same way.

13. In general, work to eliminate unnecessary e-mail, and urge others to do the same. As suggested earlier, we don't have to respond to every piece of e-mail we get. If a response isn't needed, don't send one! We should also be hesitant to send e-mail copies to people who are only on the fringe of an e-mail dialogue. While it can be a good way of keeping people informed, they may not be able to understand it fully because of not having read earlier correspondence or not having participated in earlier discussions. When they don't understand it, they'll either choose to remain baffled or they'll ask you for clarification. You don't want them to remain baffled, but it also may not be worth the time required to bring them up to speed.

There are people in the workplace who are lonely or who are looking for attention. Some of them may attempt to become your electronic pen pals. Those situations are potentially difficult because you don't want to be rude, but you also have to recognize that a series of e-mail messages which need responses can take up a lot of your time. In such situations, respond only if necessary, and consider responding with something like: "This could be a very interesting discussion, but I have so much to get done this week that I'd better not offer any further comments." Help people recognize that you are not interested in endless e-mail conversations.

In one work setting, a woman lost a magazine which she had not finished reading. She apparently set it down in the lunch room or on someone's desk or in a restroom and forgot it. When she realized it was missing, she composed an e-mail message which was fifty lines long about having lost the magazine and proceeded to send it to the entire office (over a hundred people). She felt it necessary to tell everyone how much she had wanted to finish one of the articles and why she really didn't have time to go to the library for another issue and why she couldn't afford to buy another copy that week (thus letting everyone know her personal financial woes!). If it took each person three minutes to read her e-mail message, the process wasted 300 minutes or five hours of company time—not counting the time for people to respond to her or to talk with one another in amazement that anyone would send out that kind of an e-mail message. Just because it is possible to do something by e-mail doesn't mean that one should do it!

Here are some helpful questions to ask when thinking about sending e-mail:

• Does this person need to know about this?
• Does this person have something to contribute on this topic?
• Would it be better to discuss this in person?

14. Be cautious about too quickly sending graphics and attachments. These can be a lot of fun, but they can also slow down the time for downloading messages by the recipient. While computers and Internet connections through cable and DSL are getting faster all the time, photographs still take quite a bit of time to download and require a lot of space to be stored. Send graphics and attachments to people who will really appreciate them—not to everyone you know!

15. If you send someone a lengthy attachment, let them know what portions are most important. Tell them, for example, that you especially want them to look at page 5 and page 12 of the 30-page document that you sent. Better yet, when possible, just paste into your e-mail the relevant material you want a person to examine. That makes it much easier and quicker for them to respond to you.

Spam

We've already talked some about spam, the electronic equivalent of junk mail. Many people who are connected to the Net receive a lot of it. You may receive offers to:

- Purchase a software program which will enhance your ability to make use of the Net. The program may or may not be of good quality.

- Get great deals on Viagra, breast enlargement, breast reduction, and other ways to improve your appearance and sex life.

- Purchase the services of a person to design a website or homepage on the Net for you.

- Get the very best deal possible on the next car or truck you purchase or lease.

- Purchase a book which will improve your health and lengthen your life.

- Take part in a pyramid plan which will let you make millions of dollars—though such offers almost always claim that it is really NOT a pyramid plan.

- Purchase e-mail mailing lists which you can use to send your own unsolicited e-mail marketing your own products or services.

- Visit the website with the HOTTEST, SEXIEST models anywhere on the Net. About a third of the spam most people receive is pornographic in nature.

The major Internet service providers are all concerned about the problem and are working to help reduce it. They don't want to keep people who are interested from receiving such offers, but they certainly don't want them going to those who are not interested and are offended. They also don't want sexually explicit materials going to children. Most service providers have mail controls available to parents, and it's very important to utilize those so that such material doesn't reach your son or daughter—unless you feel your son or daughter is old enough to handle the material responsibly.

As already discussed under strategy number seven earlier in this chapter, when you receive such unwanted and offensive e-mail, you should forward it to your service provider. In addition to the mail control settings available to protect children, you can also use mail controls and filters to protect yourself. These are available through your service provider or a separate software program, like Eudora Pro or Outlook Express, which let you restrict the e-mail which you receive.

You may want to consider visiting the website spamassassin.org which has a mail filter that lets you set thresholds for the identification of spam and puts those items in a folder so you can look at them if you want. You can also block future spam from the same senders. Marty ran Spam Assassin on his computer for a two-month period of time, and it identified 2,260 messages as potential spam, or 37.6 a day! During that period of time, Marty received a total of 3,061 valid or wanted e-mail messages. Spam constituted 42% of his total e-mail for those two months. Spam Assassin worked well on the whole, but it did identify as spam a few messages from people Marty knew. That is a potential problem with all sorting, filtering, or rule systems for e-mail. If you get very relatively little e-mail, you may find Spam Assassin more bother than it is worth. If you receive a great deal of e-mail, however, Spam Assassin (or other similar anti-spam software products) could become a weapon of choice.

You don't have to use a filtering system to deal with spam. The DELETE option works well with virtually all e-mail systems. Most spam is immediately recognizable from the subject line and the fact that you don't know the sender. It only takes seconds to delete dozens of unwanted e-mails. Part of the problem with spam is that it annoys us so much that we give it more thought and emotional energy than it deserves. Just delete it unread — the same way you do with junk mail received through the postal service.

And if the volume of spam has become too oppressive, consider changing your e-mail address. That's one way to get a clean start.

An extremely important caution: Curiosity may motivate you to read some of the spam that you receive. NEVER download a file which has been attached to an e-mail from a person or organization you do not know. That is an easy way to introduce a virus into your computer system and is never worth the risk. You also run the same risk when you use a link to a website which is embedded in an e-mail from someone you do not know. Clicking on that link may start downloading something to your computer from that site.

Phishing

Phishing (pronounced "fishing") is a spam technique to steal your identity — name, address, Social Security number, bank account numbers, etc. This is how it works: A technology-savvy con artist sends out millions of notes disguised as a message coming from your bank or a popular site like eBay or Paypal. The note requests verification of your name, address, birth date, account number, etc. Often the note is cleverly written to suggest that periodic updates of this information prevents fraud. A link is provided to the con artist's site that mimics the real site, logos and all. Once you've entered the requested information, you've unfortunately contributed to the theft of your identity. Using sophisticated computer technology, a piece of your identity here is combined with a piece of your identity gathered elsewhere. Before long the con artist has stitched together critical information about you, including verification of your e-mail address. With this information, access to your credit cards and bank records becomes easy.

Never, never, never click on one of these links in an e-mail message. Real companies and organizations do not ask for this information via e-mail. Only enter this kind of information on secure sites by entering the site directly from your browser.

Sadly, many unsuspecting victims are scammed each day through these phishing attacks. Marty receives about three of these a day, escaping spam filters. And the sophistication of the e-mails, including return addresses that look real, make us increasingly vulnerable to these crooks.

Developing an E-Mail Plan

Books on dieting direct you to develop a plan for weight loss. We want to suggest that you take a few minutes to think about the changes that you would like to implement in the way you handle e-mail. The following list is based on the strategies suggested in this chapter. Place a checkmark by each item that you want to implement in your own handling of e-mail.

_____ 1. Study your consumption patterns. Choose at least one day in the coming week to monitor the e-mail you send and receive.
_____ 2. Change your thinking about e-mail and the computer medium. Stay open to new ideas.
_____ 3. Control mailing lists (listservs or newsgroups).
_____ 4. Think BEFORE giving out your e-mail address. Consider getting an alternative e-mail address to use for warranties and similar purposes.
_____ 5. Enlist your friends in the process. Start talking to them TODAY!
_____ 6. Reshape your e-mailing style and set new priorities—

don't feel that you must immediately read every single e-mail you receive.

____ 7. Go through your e-mail at designated times and use a systematic approach for it. You'll find enclosed with this book a chart like the one on page 61, which can be placed by your computer.

____ 8. Keep all your e-mail except spam and phishing, and rely on the searching and sorting capabilities of your software to find things.

____ 9. Develop a consistent e-mail filing system.

____ 10. Figure out how much "neatness counts" in your company or organization.

____ 11. Never respond to an e-mail when you are angry or upset.

____ 12. Recognize that while they probably should not, people will often say things in e-mail that they wouldn't say in a written letter. Often it's better to forgive than to respond.

____ 13. In general, work to eliminate unnecessary e-mail, and urge others to do the same. THINK before you send an e-mail or copy someone on an e-mail.

____ 14. Be cautious about too quickly sending and forwarding graphics and attachments.

____ 15. If you send someone a lengthy attachment, let them know what portions are most important.

Steve's Favorite Chocolate Recipe

1. Get in the car.
2. Drive to a DeBrand store.
3. Buy chocolate.
4. Enjoy!

Those not fortunate enough to have a DeBrand store near them can go their website: www.debrand.com. (We have no connection with DeBrand and get no money from orders. We just think the chocolate is terrific!)

Chapter Six
What If You Already Weigh
400 Pounds or Have 2,000 Messages?
Rapid Weight Loss Strategies

The preceding chapter gives a solid range of strategies to help you lose excessive e-mail weight and keep the pounds off. But what if you need to lose more than a few pounds? What if you already weigh 400 pounds or have 2,000 messages? Then these crisis strategies may help you.

1. **If you have accumulated an enormous amount of saved e-mail and can't begin to process it, consider deleting everything older than a certain date.** That gives you a fresh start and leaves less for you to sort through. It's a radical step—like going under the surgeon's knife to have the extra pounds literally cut out—but in some cases it may be the best strategy. If you can't find what you want and don't have time to read it all, is it really doing you any good?

A slightly less radical step is to take all the e-mail older than a certain date and store it on a high capacity disk, thumb drive, CD or DVD (if you have a writable drive), floppy disk, or another storage medium. Then you always have the option of going through all of it to find a crucial piece of e-mail. The probability that you'll ever want that individual e-mail message enough to go through everything is, of course, not especially high.

While this counsel is especially designed for those who have accumulated too much saved e-mail, it can also be used by someone who has been out of the office for an extended period of time and finds hundreds of messages waiting. While it's riskier to delete unread messages older than a certain date, you have the consolation that many of those people are going to communicate with you again—and may already have done so with a more recent e-mail asking why you haven't responded!

Some people who use this radical strategy do a short e-mail which they send to persons whose business, cooperation, or friendship is most crucial. That message says something like this: "I regret that a substantial amount of my e-mail for the period of time from xxxxx to xxxxx has been deleted. If you wrote to me in that period and haven't received a response, my apologies! Please contact me again." Note that the explanation doesn't say that you yourself have done the deleting! In a way, this is solving your problem by creating a problem for someone else, so you should use the strategy only in the most desperate of circumstances.

2. If your e-mail software permits you to sort by sender, do so! If you can't and have a large amount of e-mail to process, then go through looking at the sender and subject displayed for each piece of e-mail. Make a one- or two-second judgment, keeping your finger on the delete key! You can go through an amazing amount of mail relatively quickly with this strategy. Steve, once confronted with 500 unread messages, skimmed through all of their senders, deleting almost 400 unread in about 12 minutes. Then those remaining didn't appear so overwhelming.

3. Identify the mailing lists, newsgroups, bulletin boards or whatever other categories are sending you the least helpful information. Start getting off those lists—right away! If you aren't sure that you want to permanently be off a list, then ask to be dropped for a certain period of time—or drop completely and send yourself an e-mail for a future date to consider getting back on the list. What if you don't have the information about how to get off the list? Try these strategies:

- Ask someone you personally know who is on the same list if he or she knows how to get off it! If you don't know someone who is on the list, obviously this strategy won't work.

- Note the e-mail address of a person who is a frequent contributor to the list. Send that person an individual e-mail asking if he or she has information on how to get off the list. This is a more considerate step than sending e-mail to the address from which you receive the list, since what you send there will end up going to everyone on the list—annoying all of them and causing them to think unkind thoughts about you.

- Send a reply to the e-mail address from which you receive the list. Put the words "delete", "remove", or "unsubscribe" in the subject line. This will do it for some lists. The list may be set up to automatically remove or delete you when that word appears as the subject. If the list is monitored (someone or a program checks mail before letting things be posted to everyone on the list), you may get a reply telling you the way to get off the list—which may involve sending another e-mail to a different address. With some lists, you should leave the subject blank and put the words "delete" and "remove" in the first line of the message.

- If those strategies fail, then join the thousands, no, make that millions, of people who have sent an e-mail to an entire list which says: "I am sorry, but I do not know how to get off this list. Someone save me! Send me an individual e-mail or post for everyone how to get removed from the list." Another possibility is to create a filter that automatically intercepts the message and sends it to the delete folder.

4. While you want to avoid overloading others with e-mail that's not needed, you may want to send the same notice to key groups of people if you are badly behind. This is a less radical notice than suggested in strategy one above (which suggests that you delete a large amount of e-mail unread). Write something like this: "I have been out of the country for the last three weeks and am slowly getting caught up on my telephone messages, letters, and e-mail messages. My apologies if I owe you a response which I have not yet made. Please be patient with me, or feel free to send me a new e-mail with the word URGENT in the subject."

5. The most radical step of all is to change your e-mail address. If you work from your home or a small business and have the flexibility, you can even change not only your e-mail address but also your Internet service provider. This means that you will literally stop receiving e-mail under your present e-mail name and address. If you are on a lot of spam lists, this is one way to stop the problem!

If you take this radical step, do one thing different than when you move from one house to another: DON'T fill out a forwarding instruction to let all your mail follow you! The purpose in changing an e-mail name is to get a fresh start. You will of course want to send a new e-mail to those with whom you want to continue to be in regular communication, letting them know your new e-mail address. **If you are going to change your service provider and if that provider is the source of your e-mail address book, then be sure to copy to a file and also to paper the contents of your address book before changing service providers.**

About that Fresh Start

Like any diet book that has counseled a crash diet, we want to remind you that getting rid of the excess pounds in the radical ways proposed in this short chapter gives you a fresh start—but is not a substitute for lifestyle changes! Study carefully the rest of this book, especially the preceding chapter on *How to Develop Lifetime Slenderness*, to learn the strategies which will help you keep the weight off and gain more enjoyment from the e-mail you consume.

Chocolate Fondue

Melt over low heat in fondue pot:
10 oz. chocolate chips   1/2 tsp. vanilla
1/2 c. light cream or half and half

Dip bite-size pieces of your favorite fruits, marshmallows, pound cake, cheesecake, pretzels or whatever you wish!

Mats Oskar

Chapter Seven
Indulging without Weight Gain
Making the Most of the E-Mail Medium

In this chapter, we share some strategies to help you take advantage of the power of e-mail. This chapter should be of special appeal to those suffering from the fear of using e-mail, who need to be gaining a little e-mail weight.

1.   Copy information to all the persons who would be interested in receiving it.   When you find useful information related to your work which is of interest to others, use e-mail to send it to them.   The ability to attach files makes it especially easy to share reports, spreadsheets, and other computer files.   Doing this can let others, including your boss, learn from the work you've done.

Remember, however, not to send chocolate if your boss is allergic to it!   In other words, think about what you send.   Simply flooding your boss and others with e-mail and attached files will not impress them with your knowledge.   It will make them want to insert a filter into their e-mail software to direct e-mail from you straight to the trash!   Send people genuinely useful material—that they'll want to taste.

Some organizations suggest people categorize e-mail by putting useful abbreviations in the subject line.   For example:

AR = Action Required.
MSR = Monthly Status Report.
FYI-R = For Your Information—Read.
FYI-K = For Your Information—Keep (but not necessarily read the whole thing at the present time).

2.   Keep people informed about your progress on a major job. This is a way to let people know you are at work on a project of importance to them, and it also provides a medium to invite suggestions and comments from them.   One strategy is to send a short e-mail with an attached file that gives the work in progress.   Use the e-mail to say enough about the attachments that others can decide whether or not they want to taste them.

While working on a book with another author, Steve received an e-mail from that author with an attached file. The e-mail read:

> *I spent the weekend revising the first three chapters. I'm attaching a folder that has all three chapters in their new form. You may want to take a look at them, though I should tell you that I'll probably make some further revisions next week after I visit with Albert. Chapter two is the one that I've changed the most thus far.*

That told Steve enough to let him make his own decision about working with the revised chapters at this time or looking at them after the next revision. Because the second chapter had a lot to do with the content of a chapter he was writing, Steve decided to go ahead and look at those changes.

3. Join newsgroups and mailing lists that will help you stay current in your field. While we have correctly identified membership in newsgroups and mailing lists as one of the easiest ways to gain excessive e-mail pounds, it's also important to remember that these groups can be very beneficial to your work. You can quickly scan a large number of responses, deleting those that have nothing of value.

Increasing numbers of people have developed the habit of trying out new ideas with people on newsgroups and mailing lists. Sometimes you'll see new strategies and opportunities discussed for the first time as part of such a group. When you have a new concept that you'd like to test with others or a difficult question for which you can't find an answer, posting the concept or question to a group can be a way to receive considerable helpful feedback. One of the greatest things about the links among people provided by the Net is the generosity with which people help one another.

Steve and Marty both posted questions about the use of e-mail, e-mail filters, experiences with service providers, and related concerns to several newsgroups, mailing lists, and bulletin boards. We received a number of very helpful responses. While it's true that some of the same ideas and problems were shared repeatedly, the very fact that so many shared them said something about their importance. In addition to that, there were some unique suggestions.

The pastor of a California congregation read Steve's request to a clergy newsgroup for ways in which e-mail was being used by the church and promptly sent Steve information on how that church uses e-mail to share prayer requests with members of the congregation. He put Steve on the church's list for e-mail for a week to let him directly experience the kinds of requests that were shared.

A chemist in Louisiana who had been hindered by a laboratory problem for months posted a question to a mailing list and received exactly the information needed to move ahead. A person needing a marketing representative in Transylvania found one through a posting to a computer bulletin board. A couple with a very sick cat got a computerized diagnosis from a veterinarian in a newsgroup, which turned out more accurate than the one provided by their local veterinarian. The cat had a rare condition that the local veterinarian had not encountered.

You can find groups relevant to your own needs and interests in various ways:

- Ask friends and coworkers for the groups they have found meaningful.

- Look for advertisements and announcements in printed magazines and journals.

- Browse through the various interest categories and chat room possibilities made available through a service provider like America Online.

- Search on the Net using words that indicate your areas of interest. Use the search engine furnished by your service provider or one like Google or Yahoo.

4. Start a newsgroup or mailing list to obtain information you need or to market your services or expertise. One way to get exposure through the Net is by setting up your own group. Your service provider will generally have channels to help you in that process. It means taking on an obligation to monitor some of the things that happen in the group you establish, but it also offers some wonderful possibilities.

5. **E-mail yourself reminders to contact others, schedule meetings, complete a major project, and meet other deadlines.** As shared earlier in this book, most service providers make it possible for you to send e-mail to yourself at a future date. That's an excellent way to be sure you don't forget something important. Obviously, calendars and personal management systems of various kinds are what most of us rely on—but receiving e-mail can serve as a strong reminder.

6. **Working on a problem in writing can sometimes help you think it through.** When upset with someone, send yourself an e-mail about it rather than that person. (To continue the food analogy, vomit on yourself rather than on your neighbor!) Use the e-mail to vent strong feelings that you aren't yet ready to share with others. Send the e-mail to yourself for review in a couple of days, by which time you may have gained new perspective.

From the start of that process, however, be sure that you address the e-mail to yourself rather than to the other person. You may remember a scene in the movie *My Best Friend's Wedding* in which Julia Roberts types an e-mail on someone else's computer that she isn't necessarily sure she wants to be sent that ends up going out as part of a batch. Don't risk that!

7. **Use copies of e-mail correspondence to document a running history of a problem you have with an internal or external supplier or service provider.** When a company was experiencing major difficulty with an outside firm that handled their payroll, the person within the company who was in charge of payroll began sending an e-mail to a supervisor each time a problem occurred. Those were saved, printed, and then sent with a strong letter of protest from the supervisor to the outside firm. It was easy to quickly build a history which was too strong to be ignored.

8. Keep in touch with friends and family in distant places and lower your phone bill. As Steve and Marty have discussed this book with others, they've repeatedly found people whose primary motivation in getting a home computer and signing on with an Internet service provider was to stay in better touch with friends and family. Time zones are sometimes hard to keep straight, and long distance phone calls can be expensive, but those are not problems with e-mail. If you're awake at two in the morning and want to send e-mail to a parent, son, or daughter on the other side of the country or the other side of the world, you can do it without any fear of waking that person up or incurring a high long distance phone bill.

Several families have developed an electronic tradition of writing updates on Sunday evening and sending them to the rest of the family. It's easy to do, and the e-mails are wonderful to receive.

You may also be able to locate long lost friends and family members using the Net. Many service providers have e-mail directories available, and you can also use search engines to look for particular people. Then you can reach out by e-mail. (There are also telephone and mailing directories available through most service providers which can help you find street addresses and phone numbers for people with whom you're out of touch.)

Instant Messaging is an option increasingly being used by people and is available through many service providers. With Instant Messaging, you have a "real time" conversation with someone else by typing notes to one another. And there are interesting examples now of telephone service being provided through the Internet. A few people have actually replaced their traditional telephone systems with those operated through their computers and the Internet.

Obviously, relying exclusively on electronic communication would be a dehumanizing process. We don't want to be like Sandra Bullock's character in the movie *The Net*—her whole existence seemed to revolve around the computer and the Internet. She played a very introverted character who rarely had interactions with people in face-to-face situations. None of us wants that to happen to us. The power of the electronic medium can, however, be used in creative ways to nurture friendships and to stay in touch with people we care about.

9.   Make new friends. Romance, love, match-making — all are on the Net! You can find all kinds of chat rooms, dating services, pen pal exchanges, and online introductions to others. You get in touch with the other person by e-mail and see if that person wants to respond. Many of these relationships go no further than the exchange of e-mail. Some become face-to-face relationships and even lifetime commitments.

Certainly you need to use caution when forming friendships over the Net, and that's especially true when those are friendships that may lead to romance. Falling in love with a person's words is not the same as falling in love with the person! And there are absolutely no guarantees that people really are who they say they are over the Internet.

Children especially need to be cautioned about forming friendships with people through the Internet. There are some predators who prowl the Internet seeking to build relationships with children. Teach your children to talk to you about anyone who tries to form a relationship with them over the Internet. Do not permit them to get together with someone met over the Internet unless you are going to be there personally to supervise.

Some of the best friendships started online aren't formed through online match-making or electronic pen pal services but rather through the exchange of e-mail as part of a mailing list, newsgroup, bulletin board, or chat room in an area of mutual interest. For people who are highly introverted, it's a relatively safe way to connect with others. Keep in mind, of course, that the deepest and most lasting friendships eventually have a face-to-face component to them.

10.   Do genealogy research on the Net and through e-mail. Many people are having a fascinating time searching for relatives and for family tree information on the Net. Increasing numbers of people are posting information about their families and encouraging others to share that information. You can communicate by e-mail with people who may be related to you or may have information about your family. There are software products and online groups to help with the research.

11. **Be cautious about ordering products or services through e-mail but recognize the value of other electronic ordering formats.** A growing number of organizations receive orders electronically. Some in fact have developed elaborate electronic ordering systems and don't even want to receive or place orders through a printed format. There are a few companies who simply won't deal with suppliers who can't handle electronic ordering and billing.

It's not a good practice to give your credit card number and expiration date through e-mail. Because your e-mail normally has to pass through several electronic gates before arriving at its destination, there is always a small possibility of someone gaining your credit information and using it for unauthorized products and services. Ordering by e-mail is easiest when you are doing it through a vendor with whom you've already established credit or who will be shipping C.O.D. If you and the vendor each have an encryption capability, that's another matter. E-mail is also an easy and inexpensive way to request further information on products and services.

Those companies organized for significant volumes of electronic ordering generally have "secure" (encrypted) ordering procedures so that you are not in danger by sharing your credit card number with them. Using such a system should be considerably safer than using e-mail. If you are at all in doubt, however, don't share that information through an electronic medium.

Chocolate Coconut Drops

2/3 c. sweetened condensed milk
1 square unsweetened chocolate
1/8 tsp. salt
1/2 c. coconut
1/2 tsp. vanilla extract

Combine first three ingredients in double boiler. Cook over rapidly boiling water until thickened. Remove from heat. Stir in coconut and vanilla extract. Drop 1″ apart on well-greased cookie sheet. Bake at 350° until set (10–12 minutes). Remove at once.

Carolyn Egolf

Chapter Eight
Designer Diets
Thinking More About E-Mail

There are three routes which may have brought you to this final chapter of the book:

- The first is that you are browsing through the pages of this book in a bookstore or while looking at a friend's copy. Keep browsing! We hope you'll want a copy of this book for yourself.

- The second is that you have read all the earlier chapters and have now come to this one. You've come to a better understanding of the basics of handling and organizing e-mail and are ready for some further concepts and issues.

- The third is that you are a sophisticated computer and Net user and therefore suspect that you are not likely to be interested in the earlier chapters. There's nothing wrong with starting here, but we hope that you'll eventually go back to the earlier chapters, especially to Chapter 5, "How to Develop Lifetime Slenderness," which shares some basic principles that are useful to virtually all e-mail users.

In this chapter, we want to consider some concepts and some issues or concerns that are potentially important but didn't quite fit in the earlier chapters. You'll find this chapter a mixed bag—dealing not only with more efficient ways to utilize e-mail but also with the power of this communication medium to improve (or harm) the quality of life.

1. Invest the time to become knowledgeable about the e-mail features available through your Internet service provider and/or e-mail software. This seems like it's saying the obvious! Of course you should become familiar with the features of your service provider and your software. But many people are not, and it's easy to fail to take advantage of those features. If you have Microsoft Outlook, for example, you can add a voting button to a message if it is going to others who have the same program. Then you can get back answers like "yes" or "no" to basic questions instead of lengthy responses. It saves time for you and for the recipients of your e-mail. You can readily see the vote count by going back to your message and clicking the tab that is marked "tracking."

Microsoft Outlook has a number of features to help you with overall time management issues which move beyond e-mail. You can create calendars, "to do" lists, and other aids.

Many people who use AOL fail to take advantage of some of the features which are very easy to use. You can set up a "Buddy List" and readily see who else is online at the same time you are, which makes Instant Messaging connections convenient. You also have access to a number of parental controls which are very helpful in protecting children. Some AOL users never think about checking the "return receipt" box which lets you know when another AOL user received your message. Other service providers and software programs have comparable features.

2. Express yourself artistically in e-mail. You can insert graphics, sound, photos, and video into e-mail, depending on the software program you are using and on your ISP. Digital cameras are becoming increasingly popular, and it is easier and easier to upload from them directly to your computer.

As mentioned previously, however, remember that some of these additions will significantly increase the time that it takes for someone else to download the e-mail and the amount of memory and storage required on that person's computer for that purpose. Thus you want to be sure that you are expressing yourself to people who will appreciate it. Your parents and other family members may be elated over the insertion of a picture of a new baby or a new kitten into an e-mail; your co-workers may be annoyed by the time it takes them to download the e-mail and by the memory it takes up.

3. Insert hyperlinks or bookmarks to Net addresses into your e-mail. This is increasingly easy to do with most e-mail software programs and service providers. You put the web address in your e-mail text highlighted in such a way that the recipient simply clicks on it and is taken to that website. This only works, of course, if the service provider of the recipient indeed provides web access. The procedure for inserting the link usually involves typing the web address, highlighting it, and then selecting an "insert link" option from a menu, pressing an icon, or pressing a couple of keys. In Eudora, any phrase that begins "http://" will indicate an automatic link. This makes it easy to direct people to websites you feel are important.

4. Use filters of various kinds to organize and prioritize your e-mail — and to keep from receiving unwanted e-mail. There are all kinds of filters available, depending on the e-mail software you use and on your ISP. The filters are of two primary types:

- There are filters that essentially transfer or copy messages to a specified mailbox within your program, to a desktop folder of your choice, or to the trash. Users of some software and ISPs may be confused by this concept because they only have one mailbox in which mail is received. Some programs, however, let you designate multiple mailboxes. Some Net users also have multiple screen names — perhaps to fit their multiple personalities :) but more often to differentiate the varied purposes for which they use e-mail.

- There are filters that primarily exist to keep you from receiving e-mail that you do not want. These don't transfer your mail to a particular mailbox or folder, but they do keep unwanted e-mail away from you. This can be a benefit to those who don't want their electronic mailbox filling up with spam.

Microsoft Outlook uses a system of internal rules to help you move e-mail to appropriate folders and block spam. This is done through their "Junk" option.

Life, of course, is imperfect, and filtering is part of life. The very complex programs that transfer your e-mail to different places for your review are not always easy to use at first. It takes time to get accustomed to them and to learn the consequences of using them. For some people who do a great deal of work by e-mail, however, the results can be worthwhile.

Suppose, for example, that you are working on a number of different projects and are receiving e-mail communication about those projects from several sources. Not all of that e-mail needs to be read as soon as it's received. A good filtering system can let you direct the e-mail for each project to an appropriate mailbox or folder, where you can read and work with it at your convenience. The programs that offer this sophistication are also designed to show that each mailbox contains unread material. Eudora Pro, Lotus Notes, and Microsoft Outlook have some of the most powerful filtering options available, though increasing numbers of software products offer some such features.

The second type of filter is less sophisticated but can do a good job of keeping unwanted e-mail away from you—and perhaps more importantly, away from your children. America Online, for example, offers mail controls which let the primary person designated for the account choose these options for each user on the account:

- Allow all mail.
- Allow mail from AOL members and addresses listed. (There is room to designate specific addresses from which e-mail will be accepted. This restriction and the next two will block a large percentage of spam.)
- Allow e-mail from AOL members only.
- Allow e-mail from the addresses listed only.
- Block e-mail from the addresses listed. (If there are those who have sent you unwanted e-mail, you can list them and not be bothered again.)
- Block all mail. (This is certainly one way to avoid spam!)
- Block file attachments. (This keeps potentially offensive attachments from getting through to children.)

America Online, Yahoo, MSN, and other service providers have other controls available to let parents restrict access not only to e-mail but also to the Net for children and teenagers.

The more complex filtering systems can be great fun to work with and are a significant benefit to those who are comfortable with them. Many people, however, will simply find the process too complicated. For the typical business and home user, the process of quickly handling incoming e-mail which is described in strategy seven on pages 56–61 of this book may be the simplest and most effective approach.

5. Remember that there is a danger in getting rid of all spam and in trying to be too slick with filtering programs. Some people set up filtering programs to automatically send to the trash all mail which doesn't have their name listed in **TO:** or **CC:**—going on the assumption that it must be spam if their e-mail name does not appear there. That's logic that works reasonably well, but it will also occasionally keep you from receiving a "blind carbon" of something. Most e-mail programs permit blind carbons, which you send to someone without having them listed on the e-mail as receiving a copy. Suppose, for example, that your boss wants you to know about some e-mail correspondence he or she is sending but doesn't want the recipient to know someone else is being permitted in the conversation. Your boss decides to send you blind carbons, but your e-mail program efficiently dumps them in the trash or blocks them from coming to you. Some people use blind carbons when sending to many people within the organization and wanting to keep the list of names confidential.

Andrew Starr from Amherst shared with us a problem that can be created by combining the sophistication of filtering with the additional e-mail strategy of autoreply. Suppose you set up a filter to put all messages containing the phrase "easy money" in the trash and to send an angry autoreply. "Then your colleague, client, or boss sends a legitimate message with the phrase 'easy money.' (If this patent comes through, we'll make easy money. Easy money could be had if our sales force were more motivated.)" Next, your now potentially former colleague, client, or boss receives an angry e-mail from you—and you haven't even read the e-mail that was directed to you. "And since many people don't know that there is even such a thing as autoreply, they assume you actually read their message and then decided to send such a response." This is not a good situation.

Here's an irony: the more you depend on e-mail for the work you do and the higher the volume of e-mail you receive, the greater the danger of trying to automatically filter out all spam. The price tag of filtering or blocking the spam is that you are likely to miss at least a few communications that you want to read. On the other hand, a person who uses e-mail primarily for personal purposes and always corresponds with the same people can rather easily block almost all unwanted e-mail. The basic filtering or mail controls available in most software packages or from most service providers make it possible to designate specific persons from whom one wants to receive e-mail and to block all others. But the more you want to receive e-mail from a wide variety of sources, the greater the problems created by filtering.

Growing numbers of people are outraged by spam. If you are in that group, you should visit the website http://www.cauce.org, which is the Net home of The Coalition Against Unsolicited Commercial E-mail. This group is taking some strong legislative initiatives to deal with spam. Service providers have been involved in several lawsuits in efforts to block spam. Many service providers encourage you to report offensive spam by forwarding to a particular address. While forwarding the offensive e-mail takes a couple of moments of time, the receipt of that information makes it easier for the service provider to block future messages from that source.

In *Release 2.0*, Esther Dyson proposes an interesting system of "sender pays" e-mail. The Internet service provider would handle most of the mechanics of this in Dyson's system. "Through your ISP, you charge $1 a message from people not listed in your personal address book or not members of communities you specify, refundable if you reply." Suppose that a friend of yours whom you've not seen for years and don't have listed in your address book locates your e-mail address and attempts to get in touch. That person would receive an autoreply from your ISP, which says something like this:

> *The recipient has an automatic charge of $1 from persons or*
> *businesses not listed in his or her address book. The $1*

*will be refunded if the recipient answers your e-mail. Is it
all right to proceed?*

Your old friend assumes you will answer and agrees to the fee.
Assuming you are happy to hear from the old friend and respond,
that fee is credited back. If you were happier not being in contact,
then you have another dollar in your e-mail account. The collection
and crediting would be done by the service providers, probably
putting the charges and credits against your monthly bill.

This system would obviously make it expensive to do marketing
by e-mail because the sender would have to pay fees in order to get
the mail delivered. That would no doubt have a beneficial impact on
the amount of spam received. While it seems as though most
households receive a lot of junk mail through the postal mail service,
that mail is expensive to send. Printing a catalog, addressing it, and
paying the postage costs enough money that only those who are well-
capitalized can afford to do so.

Making it expensive to send marketing through e-mail would
eliminate most of the low-budget and marginal operations. There is a
price tag for that though. Part of the magic of the Net has been the
reality that entrepreneurs with good ideas and very little capital could
use websites and e-mail to get in contact with people and make sales.
Dyson's system, while creative and logical, also would mean that only
major corporations could afford to do e-mail marketing at a level that
would be likely to be profitable. E-mail marketing is like postal mail
marketing in that it takes mailing to a huge number of people in
order to receive a few orders. It's difficult for people to make money
from websites alone because the site is dependent on search programs
to locate it, and many persons who would be interested will never
find the site. E-mail can help direct people to the site, where more
information is available.

The other issue is one of how your long-lost friend will feel about
being charged $1 for the privilege of sending a communication to you.
It's one thing to pay the fee for a stamp to the Post Office; it's another
thing to be charged directly by the person with whom you are
making contact. Such a system would likely also result in movie stars,
athletes, popular musicians, and other celebrities charging people for
the privilege of being in communication with them by e-mail. Those

persons might well not refund the fee if they choose to reply, and the replies would most likely be done automatically rather than personally because of the volume. That's not necessarily an argument against Dyson's concept, which we think has a lot of merit, but it would be one of the likely results.

6. **Use autoreply to handle large number of inquiries about projects with which you are involved.** While we shared an example of a problem which can be created with the use of autoreply, there are also some very positive uses for it. Suppose, for example, that you have written a report that will be of significant interest to many people in your industry and that you are eager to share the report. You can post to electronic bulletin boards and write to a newsgroup or mailing list in which you participate saying that you will send a copy free of charge to anyone who sends you an e-mail with the words "please send your report" in the subject line. If you have a program such as Eudora Pro, you can automatically have the report sent to the addresses of all e-mails which have those words in the subject line, and then you can automatically send the e-mail received to the trash or to a "requested report" folder so that you don't have to read all the requests.

In Lotus Notes, Eudora, Microsoft Outlook, and some other programs, you can use autoreply to send people a message in response to their message, saying for example: "I am out of the office until June 15. I will respond to your message when I return." Of course you don't need to use that feature if you use a laptop to monitor e-mail while you are gone or if you don't receive many pressing e-mail messages.

7. **Create a diary through e-mail.** While his son Adam was in college, Marty used a filter to save all the e-mail he received from Adam and all the e-mail he sent to him. He then printed those out, bound them, and gave them to his son at graduation. What a wonderful gift! Without the use of a filter, you could simply save each to a desktop folder at the time of reading or sending it.

While one should be cautious about printing out very much e-mail, there are times when it's appropriate to do so. Steve has maintained handwritten journals for twenty years and regularly tapes into them theater ticket stubs, restaurant receipts, letters from friends and family, and e-mails from friends and family. He doesn't save all regular letters, and he certainly doesn't save all e-mail. The journal format is great to look through and brings back warm memories. Journals and diaries work better for most of us in a paper format than in an electronic format, but the electronic medium can make it easy to create and save things for the paper medium.

8. In the development of individual and organizational strategies to make the most of e-mail and the Net, we need to remember that information and knowledge are not the same thing. Business and technology leaders talk frequently about the value of information and the importance of sharing it. That recognition is important, but it's also wise to keep in mind that not all information is of equal value. Some so-called information can in fact be wrong, and sharing it broadly will do more harm than good.

What is of a greater value than information itself is the knowledge that can be gained from that information. The words knowledge and information are sometimes used as synonyms, but knowledge implies a deeper level of understanding and usefulness. Here are some distinctions:

- The statistical results of surveys about employee morale and attitudes about work constitute **information**. The understanding about what those results mean and about the corporate changes which should result in improved morale and performance is **knowledge**.

- The sharing of facts about all the different ways people are using e-mail, which the authors have intentionally sought from all kinds of sources while preparing this book, is **information**. The determination of which of those ways should be broadly shared in a book about e-mail and the articulation of strategies to help people make the most of the medium is **knowledge** (or at least the authors hope it feels like knowledge to you). Simply binding all the books, articles, reports, e-mails received, notes of conversations, and other materials examined into a single publication would give a lot of information to purchasers, but it wouldn't impart much knowledge (and it would be at least 36 inches thick!).

- The opinions of people in focus groups about a particular project; the results of sales of the product in test markets; the advertising rates for newspapers, magazines, radio, television, direct mail, and websites; and the technical features of the product as determined by the scientific or technological staff of a company constitute **information**. The understanding of what that means and of how a comprehensive marketing plan should be developed for the product is **knowledge**.

Individuals and corporations need to think about where information needs to be shared and about where knowledge needs to be shared. Too much information sent to too many people can consume a great deal of their time without any corresponding benefit. The knowledge that is in large part derived from the information, however, generally needs to be broadly shared. The sharing of knowledge almost always increases productivity. The sharing of information can increase productivity but can also slow productivity.

That's not an argument for restricting the flow or the availability of information. It's an argument for encouraging people at every level to think in practical terms about who needs what information and about going to considerable lengths to be sure that knowledge is broadly shared (which is not the same as sharing the specific formula for a product, which may be confidential and patented—like the mysterious formula for Coca-Cola).

Organizations need to think carefully about the importance of sharing both information and knowledge in appropriate ways. Educational opportunities within organizations should help people learn how to apply information and to seek knowledge. Marty is very involved with a company called *WisdomTools* which creates story-based scenarios as learning aids for web-based instruction. Some of the most powerful scenarios help people see how to move from information to knowledge.

9. Parents need to be concerned that daughters as well as sons are encouraged to become comfortable with computers, with e-mail, and with the Net. As of the date of this writing, boys are still somewhat more likely than girls to spend significant amounts of time on the Net, to play video games, and to utilize e-mail to exchange information and thoughts with others. Trying to sort out the cultural and developmental reasons why that is the case goes far beyond the scope of this book and the knowledge of the authors.

The observation of the authors, however, is that it's very easy for parents to encourage daughters to be as involved as sons with the computer medium. Be sure girls have access; don't let boys monopolize all the computer time at home; suggest activities; make video games available which appeal to girls; and work with girls to encourage research and exploration on the Net. J.C. Herz has written a fascinating book on the video game aspect of this titled *Joystick Nation: How Videogames Ate Our Quarters, Won Our Hearts, and Rewired Our Minds.*

10. We should be concerned about access to computers and the Net for all children. Economic disparities make it more difficult for some parents to encourage their children to become comfortable with computers, e-mail, and the Net. Certainly there has been tremendous growth in the percentage of schools making computers available as a part of the learning process, but that availability is still much higher in more affluent school districts.

Parents with limited incomes find the price of a computer and the monthly fees of an Internet service provider prohibitive. Unquestionably children who have a computer available to them at home are going to become far more familiar with the medium. Our society needs programs that make computers and Net services available at far lower fees for those on reduced incomes. Libraries need to be encouraged to increase the number of computers available to the public.

Some forward-thinking companies are donating computers to non-profit organizations. There are communities, for example, in which Habitat for Humanity homes have a computer installed before the family moves in.

Steve's church has a computer lab made possible by the donation of computers by businesses in the community. A DSL connection serves all the computers in the lab. The computer lab is used in connection with a program that offers a meal, tutoring, and recreation to children.

11. Forums, debates, and dialogues carried on through the Net and e-mail offer fascinating potential for our society. Some readers of this book will remember the case of Karla Faye Tucker, who was convicted of murder and in February of 1998 became the first woman in many years to be executed. Because of a religious conversion while imprisoned, which seemed to truly transform her life, many people, including some within the prison system itself, attempted to get her life spared by the courts or by the governor of Texas (the state in which she was convicted and executed). For two weeks, Steve followed a very hot debate through a Net bulletin board. When Steve posted a couple of thoughts of his own about the debate, he discovered that not all the responses from others to him went to the bulletin board — some came directly to him by e-mail.

There are two aspects of that debate that concerned Steve. The first was that the opinions ran about two to one in favor of her execution. The second was the amount of strong emotion expressed in the e-mails. Some lines from e-mail that Steve received after posting to the bulletin board:

- "Burn, b----, burn!!!!!!"

- "She deserves to die and good riddance to her."

- "Rip her arms and legs off, and then chop her into hamburger to feed the other losers on death row."

- "You are a pathetic son of a b---- to have taken her side."

- "You dirty son of a b----. You've probably never lost someone you loved, or you'd be in favor of the murder of everyone like her."

The anonymity of the Net certainly lowers the inhibitions of people. It's very doubtful that those same people would have written letters to Steve with the same language and even more doubtful that they would have used it in a face-to-face conversation with him.

But those nasty responses do not have Steve soured on the process of online discussion. He sent a response to everyone who referred to him in terms that reflected negatively on his mother which included these words:

> *I wonder if any of us thinks through the way that we use words in the anonymous environment of the Net and of e-mail to people we don't know. You are probably a good person, but you used some language that is a problem to me. My mother died last year, and it upsets me to have people try to insult me by using language which reflects negatively on her memory. I sincerely hope that was a result of strong emotion and not really a reflection of your character.*

Steve sent those words to fifteen people, and three of them wrote back expressing their regret and thanking him for making them aware of the impact of their words on others.

He also received a large number of e-mails that were very thoughtful. Some agreed with his position and his reasoning; some challenged it; and some acknowledged that what he had written had an impact on their own thinking. While none of us has the time or energy to get involved in every online debate that is available, the process can result in an exchange of views that is healthy. The same climate that resulted in some persons feeling free to use offensive language also resulted in a candor and openness that was probably beneficial.

Many human rights organizations are making broader use of the Net and of e-mail as ways to share information about human rights violations and to encourage people to take positive actions. When a Tribunal was convened to deal with human rights problems in Bosnia, an e-mail list called *Tribunal Watch* began as a news service for activists concerned about what was happening in that country. The list expanded, and in time Tribunal Watch postings began to be distributed at the Tribunal itself. E-mail and the Net provide a relatively inexpensive way to bring together the thinking of people from all over the world.

The events of September 11, 2001 resulted in some interesting uses of the Internet, including two we'll share here. First, when many phone systems were out in New York City following the September 11 attacks, several people were still able to get in contact with their loved ones through e-mail. The Internet functions in such a way that it goes around blockages and finds alternative routes which traditional phone systems may not.

Second, those events stimulated incredible Internet activity in sympathy with those who died, in support of others, and in efforts to understand why the attacks happened. That activity came through websites, bulletin boards, newsgroups, and e-mail exchanges. People across the world were able to share in their grief because of the Internet.

12. Think about the limitations of e-mail. There is an old saying: "If a hammer is the only tool you have, then every problem becomes a nail." All of us have more means of communication available to us than e-mail, but many of our work cultures are being increasingly driven by the e-mail medium. Harry Beckwith, in *What Clients Love*, notes that it is easy to be lulled into letting electronic communication replace face-to-face interaction. That can lead to misunderstandings and also to a lack of growth in relationships.

E-mail is wonderful for many kinds of communication. Its ease of use and convenience have made it into the medium of choice for many of us. Yet we don't get the kind of nuance that comes in hearing a person's voice over the phone or even more in a face-to-face conversation where we can observe body language as well as tone.

In talking with people about this book, we discovered that many people, when faced with an awkward situation or a potential conflict with someone, will send an e-mail rather than make a phone call because it feels less threatening. But if the situation is awkward or there is a potential conflict, then it becomes all the more important not to be misunderstood. In those situations, a phone conversation is often better than e-mail; and if people are in the same city or even the same building, then a face-to-face conversation is even better.

E-mail is great for the convenient, quick exchange of information, for setting up meetings, for keeping people aware of the status of a project, and for many other purposes. If you really want to build a relationship with another person, however, an e-mail is a poor substitute for having lunch together. Chocolate tastes much better than e-mail.

Thus we want to be careful that we do not use the e-mail medium when phone contact or face-to-face contact will be more beneficial. E-mail is a wonderful, important part of our lives; but it is only one communication tool.

The Future of E-Mail

As we've worked on this book, we've had many conversations with each other and with our colleagues both about the great power of e-mail and about the limitations of e-mail. We increasingly recognize that e-mail is changing the way that we work and the way that we live.

Many of those with whom we have visited feel that spam is the greatest problem with the e-mail environment. Certainly spam is a problem, and we are both in favor of software programs, initiatives of Internet service providers, and legislation seeking to block spam. With the amount of emphasis being put on limiting spam, we think that situation will get better in time. If you want a positive analogy, think about the "do not call" lists and the dramatic curtailing of telemarketing that laws have made possible in many places.

But if all spam were eliminated tomorrow, it would not keep many of us from feeling overwhelmed by e-mail. Most of us are sending and receiving more and more e-mail all the time. While spam may annoy us, it really doesn't take an enormous amount of time to get rid of it—either by using the delete key or a filtering program. What takes more time is responding to the legitimate e-mails that come to us.

The great danger here is that responding to e-mail can become the driving force in how we spend our time in the work environment or even in our homes. Yet e-mail is often, perhaps usually, not the most important task in front of us. E-mail should be thought of as a tool more than a task. We need to keep our vision, our goals, our objectives, and our tasks clearly in front of us. We need to process routine e-mail as efficiently and courteously as we can, and we need to use the medium in a way that furthers our personal and organizational goals.

Time management systems need to increasingly recognize the role that e-mail plays in our lives. One of the reasons that we appreciate Microsoft Outlook is the effort to integrate e-mail into an overall system which includes calendaring and the maintenance of "to do" and project lists. Our suspicion is that most people are not utilizing Outlook in the way that its creators envisioned.

We're not trying to champion Outlook (or Eudora or AOL or MSN) or any other software program or service provider. We do think it is very important for each of us to determine the appropriate way to utilize e-mail in our lives so that it is a blessing rather than a curse — a means of achieving our goals and enjoying interactions with others rather than a barrier to our goals and a roadblock to relationships.

We wonder what changes may come in e-mail usage in the years ahead. Will something else replace e-mail? Will we refine the way that we use e-mail? Will we learn better ways to integrate e-mail into our overall time and life management? We'd be interested in hearing your thoughts on this topic.

If you've come to the end of this chapter and are disappointed because you had hoped to receive more advice on losing physical weight rather than e-mail weight, here are two things you can do:

- **If you're thinking about a snack, send someone an e-mail instead.**

- **Send the authors an e-mail and ask for their latest diet book recommendations!**

  martysiegel@gmail.com
  steveneclapp@gmail.com

  Or if you'd like a summary of diet books it is this: Eat less, move more!

Chocolate Snowballs

3 eggs	1-1/2 c. granulated sugar
1/2 c. cocoa	3/4 c. milk
1/4 c. butter or margarine	1 tsp. vanilla
1/2 tsp. salt	2-2/3 c. flaked coconut
1/2 tsp. baking soda	1-1/2 c. sifted all-purpose flour

Two 7.2 oz. packages white frosting mix

Beat eggs until thick and lemon colored. Gradually beat in 1/2 cup sugar. Combine remaining 1 cup sugar and cocoa in sauce pan. Add milk and butter, cook and stir constantly until sugar is dissolved and butter is melted. Remove from heat; add vanilla and salt. Pour egg mixture into a large bowl. In a separate bowl combine flour and baking soda; fold alternately with chocolate mixture into egg mixture just until blended. Fill 30 paper-lined 2-1/2 inch muffin cups half full of batter. Bake at 325 degrees for 20–25 minutes. Cool completely. Prepare frosting mix. Remove papers. Frost top, bottom, sides and roll in coconut. Let stand until firm.

Alberta Matthews

*Would you like some more self-justification
to support your chocolate diet? Here's some help. . . .*

*Some people talk about chocolate being high in caffeine.
The truth is that chocolate has 6 mg. of caffeine per ounce
compared to 180 mg. in a five-ounce cup of coffee.*

*Other people talk about chocolate having high cholesterol,
but the cholesterol comes from the added milk solids
rather than from the cocoa bean itself. A serving of
milk chocolate has 7 mg. per ounce of cholesterol; a
three-ounce serving of red meat has 70 mg. of cholesterol.*

Chapter Nine
For More Information

Angell, David and Brent Heslop, **The Elements of E-Mail Style** (Addison-Wesley Publishing Company, 1994). This book is modeled on the classic book *The Elements of Style* by William Strunk, Jr. and E.B. White. It contains a lot of material on choosing the right words and building better sentences which is certainly not unique to electronic communication, but it is also a very helpful guide.

Beckwith, Harry, **What Clients Love** (Warner Books, 2003). This is not a book on e-mail, but it is a book on maintaining successful relationships in the business world. Beckwith has some forthright comments on the limitations of e-mail.

Brake, David, **Dealing with E-Mail** (DK Publishing, Inc., 2003). This compact (72-page) book is especially designed for people who use e-mail in business settings. Brake offers 101 practical tips in an attractively illustrated book.

Dyson, Esther, **Release 2.0** (Broadway Books, a division of Bantam, Doubleday, Dell Publishing Group, 1997). The book is subtitled "A Design for Living in the Digital Age." This book may be the single best resource available for those wanting a full understanding of the digital age and its implications for business, government, and private life.

Flynn, Nancy and Randolph Kahn, Esq., **E-Mail Rules** (American Management Association, 2003). This is a business guide with an emphasis on policies, security, and legal issues. One of the authors is an attorney. This is not a book for the average e-mail user, but some corporate executives will find the extensive discussion of legal matters very helpful.

Hafner, Katie and Matthew Lyon, **Where Wizards Stay Up Late: The Origins of the Internet** (Simon and Schuster, 1996). For those who would like to better understand how the Net came into existence, this is *the* book to read.

Hartman, Diane B. and Karen S. Nantz, **The 3Rs of E-mail: Risks, Rights, and Responsibilities** (Crisp Publications, 1996). This is a solid book which looks at both the positive and negative sides of e-mail use. The perspective is primarily that of a business or other commercial organization.

Lamb, Linda and Jerry Peek, **Using E-Mail Effectively** (O'Reilly and Associates, 1995). This book would get our vote for being the best overall guide to the use of e-mail which is available. It's well written and practical.

Levinson, Jay Conrad and Charles Rubin, **Guerrilla Marketing Online, Second Edition** (Houghton Mifflin, 1997). Be sure you get the second edition. The first edition was good but so much changed that the second edition was needed. This is a solid primer for those wanting to use the Net to make money.

McFedries, Paul, **The Complete Idiot's Guide to Internet E-Mail** (Que, a division of Prentice Hall Macmillan, 1995). This is a practical "how to" book about using various software programs and service providers for e-mail. It's well written and practical, but rapid changes also mean that such books go out of date quickly.

Seeley, Monica and Gerard Hargreaves, **Managing in the Email Office** (Butterworth-Heinemann, 2003). This book was written especially for IS executives and IT professionals, but it has broader interest. Attractively illustrated with cartoons, this book covers some topics missed by others like how to work effectively with a secretary or personal assistant in our high technology time.

Sherwood, Kaitlin Duck, **Overcome Email Overload with Microsoft Outlook** (World Wide Webfoot Press, 2001). A great guide to using the e-mail features of Microsoft Outlook.

Smith, Lisa, **Business E-Mail** (Writing and Editing at Work, 2002). This book has two parts. The first deals with the basics of e-mail in business settings. The second focuses on proper business writing.

> For updates from the authors of this book, visit
> our website: www.emaildietbook.com

Other Helpful Websites

http://www.microsoft.com/windows/oe/
Official Outlook Express homepage.

http://www.eudora.com/
Official site for Eudora.

http://computer.howstuffworks.com/email.htm
Technical explanation of and terms related to e-mail explained in plain English.

http://email.about.com/
Tips, product reviews, articles, buyer's guide, offers.

http://insideoe.tomsterdam.com/
Technical information, help, and tips for users of Microsoft Outlook Express® for Windows, by Tom Koch, Microsoft MVP for Internet Explorer and Outlook Express.

http://www.cauce.org/
The Coalition Against Unsolicited Commercial Email, an all volunteer organization, created to advocate for a legislative solution to the problem of spam.

http://www.emailreplies.com/
Explains how to send effective e-mail replies, with information on etiquette; how to create a corporate e-mail policy. Books available.

http://www.fepg.net/
Helps you find the right free e-mail provider for you, from a database of more than 1400.

http://www.emailaddresses.com/
    Review of free and fee-based e-mail providers and ISPs; advice on use; discussion forums.

http://www.onlinenetiquette.com/netiquette_guide.html
    All about e-mail etiquette: offers free newsletter, articles, message boards. Upon request will send a form e-mail to someone who needs to learn about e-mail etiquette referring them to the site!

http://www.webfoot.com/advice/email.top.html
    A Beginner's Guide to Effective E-mail.

Appendix A
Understanding the Basics of E-Mail

How E-Mail Works

1. You use your computer or a similar electronic device to compose an e-mail message. You may do this using the software available because you belong to a service like Earthlink or America Online, or you may utilize software such as Eudora, Microsoft Outlook Express, or Lotus Notes. E-mail messages tend to be a little less formal and more succinct than regular mail, but the contents can be anything that you would put in a letter to send through the postal mail service. You can also attach photographs and other computer files to the e-mail.

2. Almost all e-mail software puts your *address* on the e-mail message automatically; that's the equivalent of the return address on a letter or envelope. You supply the address for the person, organization, or group to whom you are sending the message. An e-mail address contains the precise instructions needed for the mail to go to the intended recipient and no one else. It's the equivalent of name, street address, city, state, and zip code on postal mail. *No two people have the same e-mail address.* For example:

DadofTigger@aol.com

DadofTigger is the user name. This must be unique, not the same as that of anyone else receiving mail through the same organization or network. When you select an e-mail name, you are prompted to change or modify until it is unique. When Steve set up his e-mail name, all the variations on his name had been taken on America Online. His cat was sitting on his lap as he was trying to identify an appropriate e-mail name, so he decided to try "Dad of" the cat's name (eliminating the space between the words). That worked! (Tigger is not the cat's name—it's just an illustration.) Some services use numbers instead of letters, and some services assign you an e-mail name. One you've created yourself is generally easier to remember and more interesting to have.

The symbol @ is pronounced "at" when the address is read. This separates the first part of the address (WHO you are) from the second part (WHERE you are).

aol tells where you are. In this case, it's America Online, which is the service provider Steve uses.

The period (pronounced "dot" when the address is read) separates the "where you are" from the type of organization you are with (as far as receiving e-mail is concerned).

com tells the type of organization. *Com* designates a commercial business; *edu* an educational institution; *gov* a government organization; *mil* a military unit; *net* a networking organization; and *org* a nonprofit organization. Some newer addresses substitute a geographical location for the type of organization. And additional designations continue to be approved including *biz, museum, aero, coop,* and *info.*

You may occasionally see an address with an additional period ("dot") and then a two letter designation of the country. That's generally left off of e-mail addresses in the United States. For example: *ca* indicates Canada; *au* is Australia; *uk* is the United Kingdom; *jp* is Japan; and *us* is the United States.

3. Then your computer or another computer on your network puts your e-mail message into what could be called an electronic envelope and sends it out. If you are part of a network in a business, university, or similar organization and are sending it to someone else in the same organization, then your e-mail has a very short and rather direct trip. If you are part of a service like America Online, then your e-mail message travels electronically into a computer at the service; that computer in turn sends your message to its destination. Many of these electronic signals go out of the sender's computer through a modem into a phone line which carries the signals to the service

provider's computer. Electronic signals also get conveyed, however, through cables and through wireless connections. Unless you and the party to whom you are sending the e-mail message are both part of the same network or service organization, your e-mail will probably make more than one stop before arriving at its intended destination. Other e-mail computers may temporarily store the message before sending it on to its destination. All of this, however, happens at incredible rates of speed.

4. Then the recipient receives and reads your e-mail message, using software which can convert the electronic signals into a clear, comprehensible display on a computer screen. When that person has finished reading your message, he or she can respond immediately, save your message to respond later, delete your message, save your message to a file, or do some combination such as responding to your message and then deleting it.

5. If you have access to a computer, you can read your e-mail from anywhere. While attending meetings in places like Philadelphia and San Francisco, Marty reads his e-mail, accessing a computer in Bloomington, Indiana. People in places without electricity have accessed e-mail by using a laptop computer and a satellite link. People can now access e-mails through cellular phones, through PDAs, and through handheld devices called BlackBerries. This medium of communication offers marvelous flexibility. When you're away from the office or home, you can't access your postal mail so easily!

Who Sends E-Mail?

The answer is that a LOT of people send and receive e-mail, and more are being added to the electronic mail route every day. Anyone with a computer and a telephone line has the potential to send and receive e-mail—and thanks to the emerging wireless technologies, the phone line isn't even necessary for everyone. E-mails can be sent wirelessly using technology similar to that of cellular telephones. Steve recently visited with a seventy-eight-year-old grandmother who was getting ready to purchase a computer and join Earthlink to stay in closer touch with her grandchildren who live across the country and with her daughter who lives in Europe. Here are some of the people you can communicate with by e-mail:

- **People with whom you work.** This category can include your boss, your customers, your coworkers, the people you supervise, friends at work, and people in organizations of which you are a member. In many companies and organizations, task force and committee minutes are sent by e-mail. Managers and supervisors often use e-mail to send announcements, policy statements, or database or web links to large numbers of employees. People may send you copies of e-mail that they have sent to others for your information (just like people send carbon copies or photocopies of letters sent on paper). Customers may send you orders, questions, praise, and complaints. Because e-mail is so inexpensive per message to send and both fast and efficient, more and more businesses are choosing it as the preferred means of communication not only within the company but also with suppliers and clients outside the organization.

- **Your friends and family.** This is the favorite flavor of e-mail for most of us. It's great to look in your electronic mailbox and see that your parent, child, spouse, grandparent, brother, or sister has sent you e-mail. Many parents find it a very economical and convenient way to stay in touch with sons and daughters who are in college. Friends, whether in the same city or across the country or the world, often choose e-mail for the convenience and economy of the medium.

E-mail blends some of the best characteristics of a letter delivered through the mail and a phone call without some of the problems. A letter received through the mail lets the recipient read it at a convenient time, and e-mail does the same. You don't have to respond the second it comes as you do with a phone call. On the other hand, e-mail is much faster than a letter sent through the mail. When the computers or servers that process the e-mail are all working smoothly, e-mail communication can jump across the country or around the world at about the same speed as a phone call. The cost of sending e-mail is normally built into whatever small monthly fee you pay for connection to the Net. That makes e-mail less expensive than a letter through the mail service and much less expensive than a phone call (unless you start to count the cost of the computer, the modem, and the software!).

• **People you don't know** will also send you e-mail. Sometimes you'll be glad to get it, and sometimes you won't. Your e-mail address gets passed around just like the address of your home or business. People you haven't met who are interested in knowing you or doing business with you will sometimes get in touch that way. Sometimes these will be opportunities to make money.

Often these will be opportunities to be annoyed. Just as you receive junk mail through the postal service, you can also receive junk mail electronically! It comes from people who want you to buy something, donate to something, join something, or just be impressed by how clever they are. While the large Internet service providers like America Online and Yahoo are doing their best to control this flow of junk mail or spam, there are limits on what can be done. If the filtering systems they use to weed out electronic junk mail are too narrow, then you could fail to receive mail that you want.

A Harris poll, reported by the NewsFactor Network in 2003, indicated that 74% of those with e-mail favor making spam illegal. As of the printing date for this book, 37 states have passed anti-spam legislation, and there is new federal legislation. Probably all 50 states will have legislation by the time you read these words. Some of this legislation bans false return addresses and requires that sexually explicit messages be labeled. How effective legislation will be in actually preventing spam, however, remains to be seen.

America Online has aggressively sought legal remedies against purveyors of spam, particularly spam which is pornographic in nature. Microsoft has significantly stepped up efforts to fight spam.

There are all kinds of directories of people on the Net, and ambitious marketers target particular blocks of e-mail recipients. People who are very good at programming and handling electronic mail can successfully send e-mail to really huge groups of people at one time. Sending spam to a million people can cost as little as $25, which makes the temptation to do it enormous. When it only costs $25 to send an offer to that many people, the percentage who decide to buy what is offered can be very low and still result in profitability.

We also contribute to this problem when we register our e-mail addresses with various companies and organizations. Many people share their e-mail address when completing a magazine survey, when registering for a free gift at a store, or when returning a warranty card on a product. Those companies and organizations often sell our addresses to others without our direct permission. The forms we complete often have a little box we can check if we do not want our e-mail address shared, but the box is easily missed. Most of us should be very cautious about where we share our e-mail addresses. (Remember also that some people like the taste of spam. Most of us don't, but they do keep producing the stuff.)

- **People in mailing lists or groups you join** will send you e-mail—sometimes lots of it. The Net has tens of thousands of newsgroups, mailing lists, discussion groups, electronic newsletters, and other forums in which you can participate—often at no charge. These groups send you information, questions, and discussion opportunities that you can ignore, read, or answer. You can learn about these groups in printed publications, in e-mail you receive, and on websites.

Consider the math involved here. Suppose you join an electronic discussion group on "Breeding Chinchillas for Fun, Profit, and Winter Coats." (Our apologies to animal rights activists who may not find that topic humorous. There are actually no fur coats in our pet-filled households, though there once was a chinchilla.) Suppose that group has 500 participants and that on Monday morning one of them decides to send out a question like this:

Someone told me that feeding lemonade to a chinchilla will really improve the quality of its coat. I wondered if anybody has had experience doing that. It seemed to me that lemonade might not be good for a chinchilla. What do you think? Is that a crazy idea?

A group of 500 people who are all interested in chinchillas would surely have opinions on a topic like this! Suppose that seventy of them have an opinion. That plus the original question means seventy-one e-mail messages in your box—and in the box of everyone else in the group. It means a total of over 35,000 electronic messages getting sent about the question of giving lemonade to chinchillas, not including the responses to many of the responses! And that's what happens with just one such question.

Belonging to such groups can be wonderful! If you are raising chinchillas for fun and profit, it's probably a great benefit to join that kind of electronic group. You can help others, and you can receive ideas that increase your profitability. But if you simply have a pet chinchilla at your house and would not remotely consider turning the furry little creature into a pair of gloves or a hat or a part of a coat, you will probably get very tired of receiving so much electronic mail on the topic.

Steve is involved professionally in helping churches and other nonprofit organizations raise the money needed for their important work. He enjoys participating in a number of Net groups where ideas are exchanged about congregational life or about the concerns of other nonprofit groups. There have been times, however, when those groups have filled his electronic mailbox with 500 messages in eight hours—without a single one being intended specifically for him.

- **Responses to electronic bulletin board inquiries** can result in e-mail messages. Electronic bulletin boards on the Net operate much like conventional bulletin boards in the hallway of your workplace, church, school, or neighborhood store. People post things to sell, services desired, and requests for information. Since Internet bulletin boards are often organized by categories, requests for information often receive more responses than those on bulletin boards that require staples or thumbtacks.

In the process of working on this book, we put some questions on electronic bulletin boards. We were especially curious, for example, about what experiences people were having using various filtering systems to eliminate unwanted e-mail. One of our respondents had a total of 350 different filters! He provided us with excellent information.

One of the neatest things about the Net is that there are so many people who are willing to help others and who are very generous with their time and knowledge. While you may spend some time personally responding to inquiries in an electronic mail group to which you belong, you need to balance that expenditure of time with the benefit of ideas others share with you through that electronic group or in response to your bulletin board inquiries.

Creeping obesity, of course, is one of the great hazards of exploring the options on the Net. You can end up with the seams of your mailbox bulging so badly that you don't know what to do. On the other hand, if you don't try some new flavors on the Net, you may miss out on some good nutritional value. Most of us should join some electronic mailing lists or newsgroups. We need to sample them to see which ones are beneficial to us.

But whenever you join a mailing list or newsgroup, you receive information about how to drop your participation when you no longer wish to receive e-mail from that group. We suggest that you do two things with that information.

1. Copy it into a special folder on your hard disk or within your e-mail system which you title "Escape!" Then you always know where you can find the information to leave a particular group.

2. Copy the information on quitting a group into an e-mail message and send it to yourself, indicating delivery in a month. Many e-mail systems permit you to write an e-mail and then designate a future time for it to be sent. That gives you time to discover what it's like to belong to a particular group or mailing list. Then you receive your own e-mail which reminds you how to escape from the group if it isn't of sufficient value for all the e-mail you have to go through. (In rare instances, it may take more than a month to be sure how you feel about a group or list.)

For more on this and other strategies, see Chapter 5, "How to Develop Lifetime Slenderness."

Appendix B
Options in Internet Service Providers

Internet Service Providers

There are all kinds of service providers who will connect you to the Net for the exchange of e-mail, visits to websites, and for other purposes. For a few years, the number of those service providers grew rapidly. According to *Boardwatch* magazine, there were 1,447 ISPs in February of 1996 and 4,133 in August of 1997. Now we are starting to see consolidations with some of the larger service providers acquiring smaller ones. According to worldinternetstats.com, in 2002, there were still 7,000 service providers.

The fees for most services are much lower than a few years ago. In many instances you'll be charged a flat, monthly fee rather than a fee based on minutes or e-mail messages sent. In some instances, you may subscribe to a DSL or cable service for direct, fast connection to the Internet and find that it provides MSN or another e-mail service.

America Online, MSN, and Earthlink are very large Internet Service Providers. These are like the smorgasbords of ISPs. You can gorge yourself on a wide range of services, but not all those services are necessarily of value to all consumers. Steve has been a client of America Online since 1995 and essentially has a love-hate relationship with the service. It's like going to a restaurant that has a good location and your favorite foods but that occasionally has very rude or inattentive servers.

Google, the giant of search engines, has begun to offer what they call Gmail on a test basis. Though the full story on the success of Gmail will not be known until months after this book is in print, we suspect that Gmail will have an incredible impact on the industry. Google intends to provide a significant amount of storage to subscribers and to offer a powerful search engine to help users find old e-mails they want to view again, in theory making it unneccesary to ever delete a message. In exchange, e-mail is searched by computers for keywords, and targeted text advertising based on the content of e-mail messages will be displayed with the messages.

Your use of e-mail may be through an employer that maintains its own internal network which connects employees to each other and provides access to the Net. Your use of e-mail may also be through a college or university-maintained system. The quality of these connections ranges widely. Steve and Marty communicate frequently with Marty's e-mail and attached files being sent through Indiana University's connection to the Net; Steve's goes through AOL. The two of them can exchange attached files and have no difficulties with their e-mail getting through. That is, unfortunately, not the case with all college and university-based systems.

Some people have gravitated to an ISP like Juno which offers free service in exchange for your agreement to be exposed to screen displays of advertising. You complete an informational form about your areas of interest, and the advertising you see displayed presumably relates to those interests. Those with the service seem very happy with it—and particularly happy to not be paying a monthly fee. Hotmail and Yahoo also offer free Internet-based e-mail.

Many local newspapers, cable, and telephone companies are offering connections to the Net. The quality of these varies widely. Some are very good and offer helpful support if you experience problems; others are not good choices for those who are not very familiar with computers. If you use a more local service provider, you may find yourself having difficulty accessing your e-mail when you travel—unless you are willing to pay for a long distance call to connect.

Before deciding on a service provider or making a change in providers, you want to be sure to talk with other people who have had experience with the provider you are considering. Here are some questions to consider when making choices about providers:

First, how easy is the service to use? How much time is required to figure out how to send e-mails, save e-mails, use any filtering mechanisms available, attach files, or attach photographs? The big providers, like AOL and MSN, have very intuitive designs and are easy to learn.

Second, how reliable is the service? As we grow increasingly dependent on e-mail for both personal and business use, even a few hours without service can be a significant difficulty. One of the reasons that Steve stays with AOL has been the rarity with which the system is down or e-mail is unavailable. Some service providers are unavailable for hours or even days at a time, and that can be very expensive time.

Third, how easy is it to access e-mail when you travel? Are there connection numbers available all over North America or an 800 number so that you can get to your e-mail without making a long distance call? Can your e-mail be accessed via the Internet from a public computer?

Fourth, what other services in addition to e-mail are available through the service provider? Does the provider connect you to popular search engines and the web? Are chat rooms (online discussion groups) readily available? Are there other pluses available from the service provider which are important to you? What kind of quick links to news and entertainment are offered? You may be willing to sacrifice some features for a lower monthly rate.

Fifth, are there any limitations on the size of files that you can attach to e-mails? Steve has encountered repeated problems sending large graphic files to a colleague who uses MSN. If the file is large, MSN rejects it. This makes collaboration on writing projects difficult. Most providers also limit the amount of e-mail storage space users can have.

Sixth, what kind of HELP does the service provider offer? Is it easy to get on the phone and talk to a real person if things aren't working properly? Or are you stuck searching through page after page of FAQs (Frequently Asked Questions) in the hope that you'll find the answer to your particular problem?

Seventh, what kind of delays are likely to be experienced in connecting through the service provider? The reality is that we are in a time of incredible expansion in use of e-mail and use of the Net. Most service providers have had difficulty adding and upgrading equipment rapidly enough to keep up with the pace of new clients. During times of peak usage, if you have a dial-up connection with a modem in certain parts of the country, you can experience repeated busy signals before finally getting on the Net. Cable connections and

DSL connections are much better and faster, but they are also more expensive. Find out about the experiences of other persons in your geographical area before making a decision.

Index

LifeQuest is pleased to offer these important publications on the relationship of spirituality to sexuality:

Faith Matters: *Teenagers, Religion, and Sexuality* by Steve Clapp, Kristen Leverton Helbert, and Angela Zizak. How do religious faith and congregational involvement influence the sexual values and behaviors of teenagers? This book reveals the results of a national study of 5,819 teenagers representing a broad range of religious traditions, ethnic backgrounds, economic levels, and geographical locations. Includes practical recommendations for congregations and parents.

The Gift of Sexuality: *Empowerment for Religious Teens* by Steve Clapp. This book has been developed based on the research in *Faith Matters* and has been written to meet the needs of religious young people. It contains accurate factual information and clear guidance to help empower teenagers for the decisions they face about the care of their bodies, dating, sexuality, marriage, and parenting. This book has been designed for use in a variety of ways: for private reading by teenagers; for reading by teens and discussion with their parents; and for group or retreat use.

Adult Guide for The Gift of Sexuality: *Empowerment for Religious Teens* by Steve Clapp. This book has been developed to accompany the book for youth and provides helpful guidance to parents, clergy, teachers of youth, youth group advisors, and persons in the community who are concerned about teens. The *Adult Guide* includes strategies to help adults feel more comfortable helping youth in this important area of need.

A Time to Heal: *Protecting Children and Ministering to Sex Offenders* by Debra Haffner. What does a congregation do when a convicted sexual offender is released from prison and wants to become involved in congregational life? How can forgiveness and new life be offered while protecting the safety of people in the congregation? How can the faith community help persons who have been victims of sexual offenses? What can faith communities do to protect children, teens, and adults from the unknown offender?

LifeQuest, 6404 S. Calhoun Street, Fort Wayne, Indiana 46807
800-774-3360